HOW TO CULTIVATE BELONGING

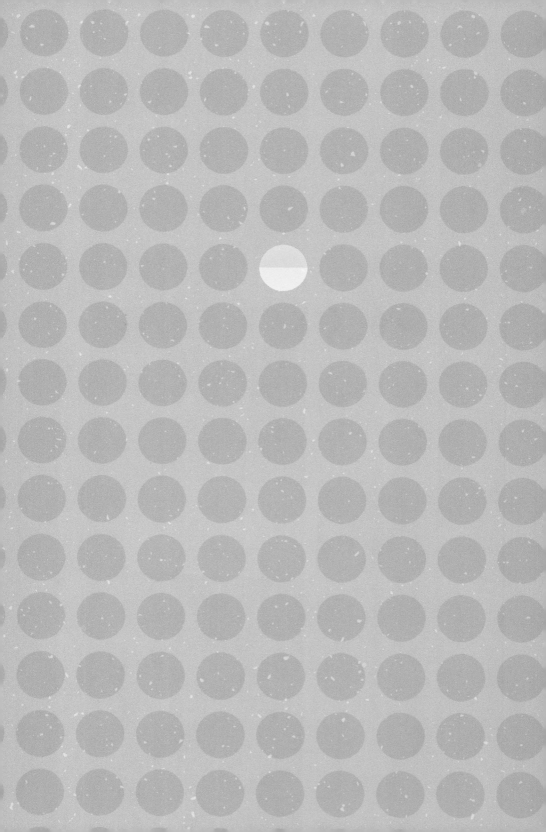

How to Cultivate Belonging

A Guide to Improving Your Relationship and Connection with Others

Adele R. Ackert, LCSW

ROCKRIDGE
PRESS

For general information on our other products and services or to obtain technical support, please contact our Customer Care Department within the United States at (866) 744-2665, or outside the United States at (510) 253-0500.

Rockridge Press publishes its books in a variety of electronic and print formats. Some content that appears in print may not be available in electronic books, and vice versa.

Interior and Cover Designer: Brian Lewis
Art Producer: Sue Bischofberger
Editor: Brian Sweeting
Production Editor: Matthew Burnett
Production Manager: Holly Haydash

Author photograph courtesy of Rachel Rivette.

ISBN: Print 978-1-64876-853-8 | eBook 978-1-64876-854-5
R0

I would like to dedicate this book first and foremost to my friends and family, whose unconditional support did not go unnoticed or unappreciated. I would also like to thank the wonderful team that made this book a reality. And last but not least, I would like to dedicate this work to all the clients I have served, both past and present: You have taught me infinitely more than I have taught you, and without you, this would not be possible.

Contents

Introduction

Congratulations on taking your first step on the journey to finding belonging! I'm thrilled that you have found my book, and I hope that you trust me to lead you along this path. Every person who picks this book up is here for a different reason, but the underlying theme is the same: How do we find belonging in this gigantic, isolating world? You may be feeling discouraged, alone, tired, or frustrated. Maybe you're more stressed or anxious than usual, or struggling with low self-esteem. This world is extremely chaotic, and unfortunately, we all have the tendency to fall into patterns that allow us to lose ourselves and lose sight of what is truly important.

At some points in our lives, we all struggle with finding our place in the world. Who do we want to be? How do we want to show up? What is our purpose? We are inundated with messages from the media, our social circle, our family, our neighbors, and our bosses and coworkers about how we "should" feel and behave. But no one is in our minds but us. Only *we* know what we're feeling and what is right for us. This book is designed to help you tap into your greatest resource—which is yourself—and develop some of the skills and tools necessary to live a healthy, happy life.

In this book, you'll find tools to address negative thought patterns, self-esteem, self-discovery, acceptance, mindfulness, goal-setting, and self-care, among others. Each chapter will walk you through these concepts and provide an in-depth look at what each one means and how it can find a place in our lives. You'll also find a series of practical exercises that challenge you to put these tools into practice. They're best when practiced regularly and incorporated into your daily routine. Don't worry about doing them perfectly the first time—all of them will take practice. Retraining your brain is just like going to the gym: You can't go in on day one and expect to lift the heaviest weights. Start slowly and accept that you won't do these things flawlessly. With regular practice, you'll get better and see the improvements you're looking for.

You may be wondering what makes me qualified to write a book on belonging. Well, first and foremost, I'm a human being. All humans need to belong and be accepted by others. We're reliant on each other for our development. We learn how to be through interaction with others. When we feel like we belong, we feel good. When we feel isolated or othered, we feel poorly, and our life starts to reflect that emotional state. Just like every other human, I have struggled with finding belonging.

We all face challenges that make us question where we fit in. Where is our place in the world? Who are we really? This is a natural and normal part of being a human. Unfortunately, finding belonging can be an isolating and arduous process, and this is where my professional experience comes in handy. In addition to being a human and struggling with belonging myself, I'm a Licensed Clinical Social Worker. I've been in the field for several years, and have worked in various environments, such as a grief and trauma center, alcohol and drug treatment, the child welfare system, residential placements for wards of the state, and private practice. I've worked with all age groups and individuals with all kinds of needs and concerns. Throughout my schooling and my work in the field, I've found one thing to be true: We all want and need to belong. My goal and objective in writing this book is to provide you with the information and tools you need to thrive—along with solidarity and understanding to help you feel that you truly do belong.

Chapter 1

Develop a Sense of Belonging

Belonging is a broad concept. We can define it and analyze it and understand it, but that doesn't mean we can feel it. In this chapter, we'll explore what belonging means and why it plays such an important role in our lives. We'll also examine ways to foster a sense of belonging in ourselves—no matter who we are—so that we can truly feel and experience it, whether at work, at home, in a group, in a community, or in a partnership. The first step in creating our sense of belonging is to do our best to understand it and why we need it.

Belonging in the World

What is *belonging*? Merriam-Webster's definition is, simply put, a "close or intimate relationship." Pretty broad, right? When I think of belonging, I tend to define it as a sense of **acceptance** for our genuine selves by another person or group of people. Human relationships are essential for us to thrive—and this doesn't just mean any old relationship. Technically, we have a relationship with the angsty teen at the grocery store who bags our groceries, or the customer service agent we have to speak with to get our Internet back up and running. However, these relationships are mindless and don't do much to nourish us—unless, of course, we put the effort in, which most people rarely do with everyday strangers. The definition states "close" and "intimate" as being key factors of belonging. True relational belonging stems from the ability to be our most authentic selves in the presence of others, to allow others to do the same, and to have a mutual, symbiotic acceptance of each other.

> True relational belonging stems from the ability to be our most authentic selves in the presence of others, to allow others to do the same, and to have a mutual, symbiotic acceptance of each other.

Cultivating a close and intimate relationship full of acceptance and respect is a lot easier said than done. If it were easy, there probably wouldn't be a book on how to do it! It does seem to be easy for some people. This can lead to us feeling like there's something wrong with us, that we're broken, or that we just don't know what we're doing. Fortunately, none of these is the case. When you think about it, so many uncontrolled variables go into creating a close and intimate relationship. Those variables multiply greatly when you try creating that relationship with a group of people.

Imagine you're back in middle school and walking into a crowded cafeteria. You don't know where to sit. As you scan the room, you spot another person sitting alone, so you decide to approach them and ask to sit with them. It's definitely scary, but not nearly as scary as approaching a group of people sitting together and asking to sit with them. When seeking out the singular person, you already know you both have something in common: nobody to sit with. Therefore, it's easier to connect and be genuine. (And if the interaction goes terribly wrong, thankfully you have no witnesses!) However, when approaching the table full of people who already have established friendships with each other, it becomes significantly more difficult to find something in common. Your mind may go to places such as, "Why would they want another friend?" "They're going to think I'm weird," or a whole plethora of other unhelpful thoughts. Thank goodness we're out of middle school, but this struggle still exists in our lives. To build an intimate relationship with one person is difficult, but to find belonging in a group is nothing short of daunting.

Belonging or Fitting In

At first glance, belonging and fitting in may seem like the same thing, but there are some key differences between the two. When two or more people have an intimate connection based on their genuine selves, that's belonging. *Genuine* is the key word here. We can't truly belong if we're not our most authentic selves. This can mean connecting through our **values,** or through interests and hobbies—but the connection has to be genuine.

Fitting in, on the other hand, does not require us to be our most authentic selves. In high school, I dressed a certain way and wore my hair in a particular style because I wanted to fit in, but that doesn't mean it was necessarily what I wanted or liked. When we conform to norms that have been created by others because we don't want to be the odd person out, we're striving to fit in, not belong.

> When we conform to norms that have been created by others because we don't want to be the odd person out, we're striving to fit in, not belong.

For instance, I work with a client who has absolutely no trouble fitting in. He's a class clown, very charismatic, and extremely likable with his peers. However, he maintains that this isn't his true self, which he hides beneath a facade. He says that in reality, he feels disconnected and isolated from his peers despite being well liked and, by all means, popular. Most of us are familiar with this situation. We may feel like we "belong" in a group because we have molded and shaped ourselves to fit the so-called requirements of a group. That disingenuous sense of belonging is actually fitting in. When we're able to find a person or group of people who connect with us and accept us for who we really are—while not making us conform to any norms or regulations other than being ourselves—that is when we truly belong.

Another example of fitting in, but not necessarily belonging, came from a client of mine who was the only Black woman in her friend group. The topic of blackface came up in a discussion with her friends, and while no one directly defended the use of blackface, my client was the only one to speak on the trauma associated with that act and how it perpetuates harmful stereotypes. My client told me that her friends agreed that it was bad *today*, but that the use of blackface historically in film and comedy wasn't necessarily a bad thing—because people in the past were "of a different time" and "didn't know better." My client had a very different perspective, largely informed by her existence as a Black woman. This situation led my client to a values clash: She could either agree for the sake of fitting in (but not truly belong) or she could disagree and speak her truth (and neither belong nor fit in). She went with the latter, and while this did result in a lot of hurt feelings and further struggles down the line, she never regretted it. She always maintained that she doesn't want to fit in with people with whom she does not share the same values or beliefs. Fitting in is not always true belonging. When we are able to be our genuine selves with others—and others with us—then we can find belonging.

The Role of Technology

We live in an era of attending Zoom meetings, making FaceTime calls, admiring friends' and influencers' beautiful Instagram photos, and talking with like-minded strangers on Twitter. One could easily argue that technology builds connection and belonging, and they would absolutely be correct. Technology connects us with so many people. There are Facebook and Reddit groups out there for every single person to join, no matter how uncommon their interests may seem. Technology provides us with a way to reach out to people and feel accepted and validated and have a real sense of belonging.

For some, technology has been the only way they've been able to find a sense of belonging. Interacting with people in person is extremely difficult for many, and impossible for some, for all kinds of reasons—chronic pain, severe mental illness, age, language barrier, disability, or social phobia, among many others. It is infinitely easier and much more convenient to connect with others and find a sense of belonging without ever leaving the comfort and safety of your own home. This is a perfectly valid way of finding connection and belonging, and we are fortunate to live in a world of technological advancement, where the ability to get most of our interpersonal needs met is at our fingertips.

However, as great as technology can be for bringing us together, it can also have the opposite effect and drive us apart. How many of us have ever gotten into a Facebook fight with a relative over politics and inadvertently made Thanksgiving dinner really awkward? How many of us think that if we have to do one more Zoom call, our eyeballs will melt out of their sockets? The reality is that interaction is draining, especially when it isn't fun or isn't with someone we agree with or connect to—and people we don't agree with or connect to are all over the Internet! While we have the capability to connect through technology, sometimes the best thing we can do is disconnect from our online profiles and reconnect to our environment and ourselves.

A Sense of Loneliness

Loneliness is an all-too-common emotion, and one that most of us try to avoid. By trying to avoid this emotion, we sometimes fall into the trap of just fitting in. However, it can be very easy, while striving to fit in rather than belong, to end up still feeling lonely, even when we're surrounded by people. This is because we're not feeling seen or validated for who we are. We try so hard to find that sense of belonging that we sacrifice our unique, wonderful selves in the process. Despite possibly reaping the benefits of fitting in, usually we don't end up feeling fully actualized.

> By engaging in behavior that aligns with our values, we can reduce the feeling of loneliness because we have learned to support ourselves.

Being alone does not necessarily mean feeling lonely. We can feel lonely and not technically be alone, and we can also be alone and not have to feel lonely. Loneliness is an emotion associated with feeling isolated—which doesn't necessarily mean *being* isolated. For instance, many introverts love having ample alone time to recharge. They don't feel lonely because they're using their time to value and affirm their true selves. By engaging in behavior that aligns with our values, we can reduce the feeling of loneliness because we have learned to support ourselves. Likewise, we can also attract others into our lives who see us for our true selves and value us just the same.

Biology of Belonging

Humans' need to belong has evolved over time, just as our society and relationship structures have. Our first instances included belonging to a tribe. When humans were solely hunters and gatherers, it was nearly impossible to survive, let alone thrive, outside a group. Our very early ancestors depended on one another to protect against predators and enemies, effectively hunt large animals, raise children, tend to crops, and so on. All of our basic instincts are designed to keep us alive.

One of our core biological needs is to ensure survival—and our dependence on others helps increase our likelihood of survival. In other words, our very survival has been evolutionarily linked to depending on other people.

We need other people not only to ensure our survival as individuals and as a species, but also for healthy development. Human babies are probably the most feeble and needy offspring on the planet. (Any new parent will agree!) When we're born, we can't stand, run, feed ourselves, or even hold our head up. Everything we learn, we learn from social interaction. Many of us have heard of feral children. These are children who have been raised with little to no social interaction and have suffered extreme neglect. Although some feral children have made monumental strides in their development through various forms of therapy, many will never be able to learn to use the toilet, speak, feed themselves, or walk upright. Russian professor of psychology and doctor M. M. Reshetnikov states, "Healthy brain is a necessary but not sufficient condition of development and adequate functioning of human mind. Feral children have functional instincts and reflexes, which are genetically determined, in contrast to conscious activity that is an acquired function, developing only in social informational environment." Essentially, to develop properly, we need more than just a fully formed and functional brain; we also need people.

However, not just any person will do. We need bonds with people who are positive and offer a low level of conflict. According to researchers Roy Baumeister and Mark Leary, having a relationship with another human who has high levels of friendliness and low levels of conflict can improve our lives in various ways. By interacting with such an individual—whether at the age of five months, five years, or fifty years and beyond—we develop long-term bonds.

Belonging can positively impact the development of our cognitive abilities and emotional intelligence. By interacting with others, we learn how to treat others, what is expected of us as humans, the difference between right and wrong, and generally how to function in modern society. Humans are highly goal motivated, meaning that our biological drive to belong serves a purpose. Sometimes that purpose is the development of our physical selves, our cognitive selves, or our emotional selves. Sometimes the purpose is just for pleasure. Regardless of the purpose, belonging meets a biological need that has been within us from the very beginning of our history.

Belonging also assists in the regulation of our behavior and emotions. We're likely to react to stimuli differently based on whether we're with a group or by ourselves. Likewise, we react differently when we're in a group where we belong compared with one where we don't. Therefore, the amygdala (the emotional center of the brain) reacts differently to situations based on whom we're with. This is partially due to the adverse effects of judgment, along with the protective factors of belonging. For instance, if we're with a group of friends, we're less likely to get into a bar fight than when we're by ourselves (unless our friends encourage that kind of behavior, which is a whole different topic!). Our friends are likely to step in and help us access our regulation skills. Similarly, being in the presence of a group we belong to reduces stress and negative emotions in general. Also, if we did indulge our aggression and proceed to fight with a stranger in a bar, our friends might judge us negatively and determine that we're no longer a fun or good person to be around. The influences of belonging to a group help us use our regulation skills more effectively to avoid the possible negative consequences.

Unfortunately, there can be many obstacles when it comes to our journey toward belonging. These can further increase our sense of loneliness and feelings of solitude and isolation. Some of these factors include race or ethnicity, immigration status, ability, neurodivergence, gender identity, sexuality, size, socioeconomic status, and age. While these factors make us unique and are not negative things, in certain communities or situations they can also increase feelings of isolation. This can create increased difficulty when it comes to finding a sense of belonging and developing a healthy, supportive community. This is not to say it is impossible, but diversity, while an incredible asset, can also offer unique challenges when it comes to belonging in some communities.

Benefits of Belonging

Humans by nature feel the drive to belong. We covered the "why" in the previous section, and here, we'll discover why it is so important to us as humans to belong and what reinforces our need to belong. Many needs are met by engaging in groups and partnerships as a human. First, and most simply, it makes us feel good. Being accepted by a group or another person makes us happy, and we as humans love being happy. When our personhood and identity, which are often tightly locked up inside us, are seen, accepted, and validated by another person or group of people, we feel a sense of "Oh, I'm normal and people like me." And who doesn't want that? It feels good to belong.

Belonging to a group of people—a group of friends, a support group, an organization, or a team—can significantly increase feelings of happiness. We're all seeking the same reassurance that we're not the outlier. Among the most common questions clients ask me are "Is this normal?" and "Do other people struggle with this, too?" When people are seen and validated in this way, they often visibly relax in a session. This also changes the way we think. If we know that we're not alone in a struggle, we judge ourselves less. There's a group on Facebook for everything—every situation, illness, experience, interest, and belief. By belonging to groups, virtual or in person, we can get that sense of belonging. We stop thinking that we're "crazy" or "weird," and we begin to think that maybe we do belong. By feeling less isolated in that way, individuals often begin to relate to their thoughts differently. This offers people an opportunity to challenge negative thought patterns and reduce judgmental thoughts toward themselves, which leads to greater feelings of general happiness.

Various forms of social support can provide great relief for someone dealing with grief, anxiety, stress, depression, or addiction—the list goes on. A quick Google search will show local in-person or virtual groups that offer support. Most people are familiar with the countless groups that offer support for addiction and substance use. We may be less familiar with grief or other support groups, but there are a slew of them in most communities, as well as online. And there is a reason these groups are so prolific: They work. The Mayo Clinic has noted that finding a sense of belonging in a group is a major factor in reducing stress and anxiety. The theories behind these groups account for a significant percentage of their success, but most important, they provide a safe space to talk about one's experiences and to feel connected to others. None of us exists in a vacuum, and by engaging in support groups, we're able to validate our experience, learn new coping strategies from others, interact with peers and equals, and gain appreciation for their experiences and struggles.

Having a sense of belonging can also be a protective factor when dealing with and recovering from trauma. I once worked with a brother and a sister, close in age, who had undergone some severe trauma. The girl belonged to many extracurricular groups in school and had a solid group of friends. She wasn't left entirely unscathed, but because of the support of friends, teammates, and teachers, she was able to navigate through her trauma in a way that did not lead to any disruption in her grades, self-esteem, relationships, or general ability to function. Her brother, though, was much less engaged in clubs or sports, and he had far fewer friends. After experiencing the same trauma, he began to experience poorer grades in school, struggled with his relationships, and began having behavioral problems in school and at home. While the sister reported feeling supported in her healing process, her brother reported feeling isolated. Both children were as similar as possible in their experience before and after the trauma, but both reacted completely differently, largely because of the difference in their support systems and sense of belonging.

Belonging to a group isn't just helpful for dealing with mental health struggles; it can also be helpful in practical matters in school or work. Most people feel that they benefit from belonging to a study group or consultation group at work. They can process situations in a group environment, learn new things, and receive training and support. Belonging to a group like this also helps with motivation because it can provide a person with peers who can hold them accountable and provide encouragement.

How This Book Will Help

The purpose of this book is to guide you along your journey to finding belonging in the world. Throughout, I'll provide various tools and skills to assist you in becoming your best self and finding belonging in this crazy world. My goal is to help you feel validated and to provide the tools to help you thrive and be your most authentic self. The exercises are designed to challenge you. They'll require you to be introspective and open to learning new things and possibly changing your mindset. We can't produce a different result if we keep doing the same things, after all! Some of this is a learning process and will be uncomfortable, but remember, you're growing! Growth isn't always the most comfortable feeling, but it is rewarding.

Specifically, this book will cover topics such as acceptance, **self-compassion**, the benefits of positive thinking, cultivating a growth mindset, developing strong self-care techniques and routines, and cultivating positive connection. All of the following chapters are designed to foster your sense of belonging. The tools found in each chapter will challenge you to put these concepts into practice and evaluate how you can apply them in your daily life.

I'd also like to add a disclaimer before we dive into the real work: I am by no means an expert on *you*. You're the only one who is an expert on what you specifically need. I can't take this journey for you; what I can do is offer you a hand to guide you through the process. I'm just another human trying to navigate the complicated art of belonging and the unique challenges that our current society offers. I just happen to have some additional training on the subject. I'll use my training and knowledge to give you the tools you need to cultivate belonging in your life. It's up to you to use them. It's my hope to provide you with everything you need to improve your life and your sense of belonging so that you may reap the profound benefits that belonging offers. I also hope that you'll be able to use those tools to help others—belonging is dependent on good people, and by being a good person, you can make the process that much easier for someone else.

Key Takeaways

- Belonging means being accepted for our genuine selves by another person or group of people.

- Humans need positive interaction to appropriately develop and thrive.

- Humans are hardwired to want to belong and to avoid rejection.

- Having a sense of belonging can provide many great psychosocial benefits.

- Sometimes we have to change our mindset or behavior to seek out true belonging.

- This book offers tools and advice on how to cultivate belonging.

Chapter 2

Embrace Acceptance

Now that we've covered what belonging is, we can move on to the concept of acceptance. We'll cover what exactly *acceptance* means, how and why it is a useful tool in our journey toward belonging, and how we can implement it in our daily lives to help us manage difficult emotions and uncomfortable situations. We'll cover some practical exercises that will help you put acceptance into practice, with examples that illustrate how you can embrace acceptance in your day-to-day life.

What Is Acceptance?

Acceptance can be difficult to define without using the word in the definition. For me, it's easier to start with what acceptance is *not*. Acceptance is not agreeing, cosigning, or settling. Acceptance is not being in a bad situation and saying, "I accept this and this is fine," and then never leaving that situation. Acceptance is not complacency or staying stuck. The best way I can define acceptance: the acknowledgment of a situation or circumstances, along with the acknowledgment of what can and can't be changed. Acceptance connotes a degree of moving forward. We acknowledge a situation, and then we take the next step. Sometimes that step is to leave the situation if possible, and sometimes the next step is to endure and cope if nothing can be changed.

My favorite example that illustrates why acceptance can be so powerful involves dealing with traffic, which is something almost all of us can relate to. I grew up in a small town in the Midwest, where traffic was just not a thing. Once I moved to the suburbs of Chicago, traffic became an everyday occurrence. Not only was I not used to it, but I also found it immeasurably frustrating. During my first two years in the suburbs, I worked retail at a store 20 minutes away from where I lived, on a good day with no traffic. I also had a boss who was not the easiest to get along with, nor the most flexible. The worst part was that I often had to start work right at rush hour, so traffic was a monster. Every day, I would drive to work and inevitably get stuck in traffic. My anxiety would skyrocket because I would tell myself that I'd be late for work and probably fired. I'd scream at other drivers who were in the exact same position that I was. It became such a stressful part of my daily routine that I found myself getting sick with anxiety every day before I left for work. My anxious brain cycled through these thoughts: (1) I will get stuck in traffic, (2) I will be late to work, (3) I will get fired, (4) I will have no money and have to drop out of grad school and live on the streets.

One day, with the help of my therapist, something clicked in my brain and I realized I can't change the traffic. The traffic remains the same, day in, day out, yet I was reacting to it in such an extreme way and causing myself so much anxiety, anger, and dread. I could not control the traffic no matter how hard I tried, how loudly I yelled, or how furiously I punched my steering wheel. What I could change, however, was how early I left, whether I checked the traffic update to make sure I had enough time to get to work, whether I took deep breaths when I was feeling anxious, and whether I acknowledged that I wouldn't be destitute if I was late to work once, even if I was fired, which was unlikely and unreasonable. (By the way, I was late a total of three times in my two years of working there, and I was never fired or even castigated.)

A lot of people's brains work like this—it's a way to protect us from possible negative situations. We can thank our ancestors for being hyperaware of things going on around them. For them, it was a survival mechanism, but for us, it's at best unhelpful and at worst downright damaging to our well-being. Our anxious brain is so concerned with keeping us safe that it sometimes fails to keep us healthy. By accepting that I couldn't change the traffic—only my response to it—I reduced so much anxiety. My anxious brain created situations in my head that were not even real, let alone likely. I made the decision to accept the things in my life that I couldn't change and to change the things I could. By trying to control what I couldn't, I gave myself unnecessary stress. Life is full of stressors, and it's okay to be annoyed or frustrated with things we can't change—but we don't have to make life any more difficult on ourselves than it already is. That is acceptance.

Why We Should Embrace Acceptance

Acceptance isn't just about accepting situations or circumstances that are out of our control. It's also about accepting ourselves and other people. I think most of us are painfully and consciously aware that we can't change other people, as much as we wish we could sometimes. But too many of us still get caught up in situations in which we're desperately trying to "make" another person do something or change their behavior.

Let's say you have a friend who is in an unhealthy or abusive relationship. To be a good friend and to live according to your values, you feel like you should make your opinion known, which is perfectly acceptable. Unfortunately, the friend doesn't listen to you and stays in the relationship. Should you try again or let it go? Sometimes letting it go can feel as if we're giving up or like we're okay with the situation, but this isn't true. If we keep telling our friend each time we see them that we hate their partner, what will that do to our friendship? Those of us who have been in this situation know that it typically only creates more problems and leaves our friend, who is in a vulnerable situation, without a safe space.

By voicing our opinions to our friend, saying what we feel once or twice but explaining that we'll respect their decision, we end up doing a lot more for those we love. We give our friends the autonomy and respect to choose. We don't have to love their decisions—we have to love the person. This can strengthen our relationships and also relieve us of the responsibility of managing other people who don't want or need to be managed. Not to mention, by trying to control other people, we ultimately set ourselves up for failure because it can't be done no matter how hard we try. We can't simply try harder than the other person and expect them to change.

> We don't have to love their decisions—we have to love the person.

We're also allowed to set boundaries when we have a loved one who is engaging in behavior that we don't love. Using the same example, perhaps you don't think it's healthy for you to hang out with your friend while they're still in this unhealthy relationship. Maybe it's too draining to your emotional energy or it's hurting your friendship. It's perfectly okay to say that you need to maintain some distance for a while because of the unhealthy relationship. This isn't you trying to force them into doing something they're not ready to do; this is you standing up for yourself and your well-being. It's easier said than done, but it's a whole lot healthier to set those boundaries to protect and respect yourself and your well-being than to have fluid boundaries where you sacrifice yourself and alienate your loved ones even further.

One of the hardest lessons I've had to learn as a therapist is that no matter how hard I work, it doesn't mean a client will change their behavior. People have to want to change and improve. We can't force them to be ready or to take those steps; we can only control what we say and how we respond to behavior. So much internal conflict is created when you try to change another person. You get frustrated because they're not changing, and you also end up expending a lot of emotional on energy on something that's out of your control. We also can create conflict with others by trying to make them do something they're not ready to do or don't want to do. By accepting our lack of control in these situations, we free ourselves of the burden of trying to change something that's out of our hands. We no longer set ourselves up for a losing battle, and we acknowledge and accept that it is also not our battle to fight.

> By accepting our lack of control in these situations, we free ourselves of the burden of trying to change something that's out of our hands.

The same tenets are applied to things about ourselves that we don't like and would like to change. We can't force change if we're not ready, but what we can do is look at ourselves with compassion and exercise a growth mindset. We'll delve further into these concepts later; right now, we'll focus on the language we use with ourselves and on keeping acceptance at the forefront of our minds.

If we're not happy with our weight, for instance, we may say things like "I'm so fat—no one will ever want me," "I'm ugly," and so on. These words make us feel worse and are generally not very motivating. When we approach the same situation from a place of gratitude and acceptance, we may say things such as "I may not love where I'm at in my journey right now, but I have the power to change." By accepting where we are, we don't have to love everything about that situation. We can approach it from a place of neutrality. What we're doing is acknowledging that maybe we're not where we would like to be ideally, but we can make changes that will get us closer to our goal.

By reframing those thoughts, we set ourselves up to feel happier and more motivated, and we're less likely to get stuck in negative thought cycles. We shift our thoughts from the uncontrollable (what other people think) to the controllable (what we can do about the situation). The use of reframing can interrupt the **negative thought cycle** and allow our mind to explore alternative options, rather than just the negatives. Our negative thinking is kind of like a hamster wheel: It keeps going as long as we allow it to, but at some point, we've got to get off. By choosing to get off that wheel, we can look at things through an alternative lens. This allows us to move forward rather than getting stuck.

Battling Uncomfortable Feelings

I'll be the first to tell you that life is not easy, and neither is acceptance. We're going to feel uncomfortable feelings throughout our life journey and through our quest to practice acceptance. Discomfort is inevitable: This is the first thing you need to accept. The second thing you need to accept is that joy, love, comfort, and happiness are all inevitable as well. Understanding that our baseline as humans is not "happy" is the first step to practicing acceptance. Our baselines vary from person to person, though they typically hover somewhere around neutral to content. From that jumping-off point, life will take us on a roller coaster of a journey down to the pits of despair, up to the peaks of euphoria, and everywhere in between. Acceptance and coping are not about getting rid of those feelings, because feelings are neither good nor bad; rather, coping skills and acceptance can help make the emotional experience more tolerable. Think of your emotions as road signs rather than roadblocks: They aren't there to stop us but to show us where to go and how we need to proceed.

> Understanding that our baseline as humans is not "happy" is the first step to practicing acceptance.

By seeing our emotions as useful and informative, we can approach them with curiosity instead of fear. Feelings are not to be avoided—they're to be experienced and felt, even the uncomfortable ones. We as humans spend a lot of time trying to avoid discomfort that is inevitable rather than trying to find healthy ways to cope with it. The way I see it, our life stressors are divided into two distinct categories: inevitable stress and self-imposed stress.

Inevitable stress includes those things in our life that we can't avoid, such as major life transitions (births, deaths, work, marriage, etc.) and minor everyday occurrences (flat tires, paper cuts, weather, long lines at the store, money problems, etc.). These things in life are normal and inevitable—and will often include aspects that are largely out of our control. Self-imposed stress, on the other hand, stems from how we react to these situations. We significantly prolong our suffering if we obsess over something we said in a work meeting that our boss didn't agree with, how it ruined our whole day, and how we shouldn't have even said anything to begin with. We create more stress for ourselves when we beat our-selves up and think about every possible way we could have avoided that inevitable stressor—which is no good, because unfortunately, no one has yet invented time machines. There is no changing what happened, so we might as well accept it, deal with it, and move on, as well as try to learn from it in the future. We aren't robots, and we are going to make mistakes. The least we can do is not beat ourselves up over those mistakes.

Plenty of scenarios and emotions make acceptance very difficult. For instance, feelings of self-worth, inadequacy, and hopelessness can be very difficult to experience and accept. I think the key is accepting the feelings as valid but the result-ing thoughts as untrue. Our feelings and thoughts are very interconnected, and they can play off one another.

For example, what thoughts do you have when you're feeling lonely? For me, those thoughts include things like "Nobody likes me," "I'm not a good friend," or "I have no personality." These thoughts definitely do not make me feel any better or any less lonely! It's okay to feel lonely and we can validate those emotions for ourselves, but we don't necessarily have to validate our thoughts. We can reframe our thoughts by simply remembering what they are: words in our heads. They're not necessarily true, they're not always helpful, and they definitely don't always need to be paid attention to.

We may not be able to control what thoughts come into and go out of our minds, but we can control our response to them. Instead of feeding into the cycle of negative thinking, we can tell ourselves, "I am having the thought that nobody likes me." This depersonalizes it, creating distance between ourselves and the thought. We're no longer stating that thought as fact, so the brain does not respond to it as a fact.

I encourage you to reflect on ways that you perpetuate your own negative thinking and how you can use this concept to stop that hamster wheel.

> We cannot control our thoughts, but we must realize that our thoughts don't have to control us either.

Because our mind is wired to focus on the negatives (keeping us safe but not necessarily healthy), it may try to trick us into rejecting acceptance. This is perfectly normal and okay. My coworkers and I often talk about acceptance and how we may know all the tricks but sometimes we just don't want to use them. I encourage you to sit with that feeling. Ask yourself why you're having the thought that acceptance won't work or that it's dumb or pointless. Use those same concepts discussed previously to approach those thoughts. "I'm having the thought that acceptance sucks." That's okay. You're allowed to have that thought. Sit with those feelings and try to approach them from a place of curiosity. What is your mind trying to tell you? Where is that resistance coming from? What is your brain trying to protect you from? Do you even need protecting?

By challenging these urges of nonacceptance, we can slowly but surely rewire our brains to be more positive (or at least neutral). We don't have to feed ourselves constant negativity. We don't need to prolong our suffering or create more stress for ourselves. We cannot control our thoughts, but we must realize that our thoughts don't have to control us either.

Belonging Toolbox: Reframing Negative Thoughts

This exercise challenges you to more closely examine the emotions that you feel, the negative automatic thoughts that happen as a result, and how to reframe those thoughts. It will give you practice noticing and accepting your feelings, calling out the negative thought patterns, and then reframing those thoughts to be more helpful and less judgmental. I'll provide a few examples to show you how it's done. You can then pick some common emotions for yourself, write down what your automatic negative thought is, and then work on a reframe.

EMOTION	NEGATIVE THOUGHT	REFRAME
Happy	This isn't going to last.	Uncomfortable feelings don't last either, so I will enjoy happiness while it's here.
Worthless	I am no good.	I'm having the thought that I am no good, but I know that I am a unique and valuable human being.

1. What did it feel like to try to reframe your negative thoughts? What did your mind try to tell you about that process?

    _____

    _____

    _____

    _____

    _____

    _____

    _____

    _____

2. What challenges or obstacles may prevent you from practicing acceptance?

    _____

    _____

    _____

    _____

    _____

    _____

    _____

    _____

Everyday Acceptance

Our lives are filled with situations that are beyond our control, both big and small. We are inundated with news of global conflict, and it may feel overwhelming to be aware of how little we can control on a global scale. This can feel very disheartening. However, if we continue to focus on what we can't change, we lose sight of the things we can. For instance, if we're not happy with the political climate, we personally cannot overhaul the government, but what we can do is advocate, vote, and educate and encourage others. Those are the actions that create lasting change. It may not feel like "enough" at times, but it is important to focus on your own personal values and ensure that your actions align with those values. By not accepting situations that are out of our control, we can find ourselves discouraged and hopeless.

Another very common example of using acceptance is weather. Growing up in the Midwest, I learned very early never to rely on the weather or any weather reports. We can decide to notice it is cold and rainy and go on and on about how annoying it is and how it ruined our whole day, or we can acknowledge and accept the weather for what it is, adjust, and move on. Humans are incredibly adaptable as long as we don't allow ourselves to stay stuck—which is what we do with nonacceptance. By not practicing acceptance, we can easily find ourselves trapped in a web of misery, trying to fight our way out. However, acceptance is like quicksand: The more you fight against it, the faster you'll sink.

We're faced with situations every day in which we can practice acceptance. We want to analyze a given situation in a few different ways to determine how to handle it. No matter how we proceed, acceptance is at the root of all our choices. The first question you want to ask yourself is "Can I change this situation?" A flat tire you can change, but a thunderstorm you can't. The second question is "Can I change my attitude about this situation?" We can absolutely see a thunderstorm as a good thing if we change our perspective, but we will always see our friend in an abusive relationship as bad. If we answered yes to either of those questions, it's time to act. If we answered no to both, we need to employ something called "radical acceptance." This is a term coined by Marsha Linehan, an American psychologist and creator of the widely used and successful methodology called dialectical behavior therapy. Radical acceptance means that we acknowledge that we truly cannot do anything about the situation and accept our feelings as being valid and important, even though they may not be comfortable.

I have personally learned a lot of lessons in acceptance through my clinical work with teenagers. I previously worked at a group home with teenage girls who were all involved in the child welfare system. Frequently, the girls at the house would run away to see their boyfriends or just get away from the confines of the house. Usually, we knew when a girl was planning to run. I and most of my coworkers would plead with her to change her mind and stay. We did everything (we thought) in our power to prevent the run, and it never worked. I decided to change my tune and practice acceptance.

One of my clients was on the front porch, backpack packed and ready to go. I went outside to talk to her. She was angry, so she didn't respond. I let her know that it was obvious she was going to run and that I wasn't there to try to stop her. I explained that I really, truly hoped that she didn't run away, but I understood that it was her choice. I told her I hoped that she would at least be safe and that my door would be open whenever she returned to the house. By taking that approach, I built connections with the girls in the home and improved our rapport immensely. They saw me as someone they could turn to, in good and bad, and they trusted me even more. Realizing that I couldn't control their actions—only my response—made me a better therapist and support system. It also reduced my negative feelings toward the girls and the situation as a whole.

Belonging Toolbox: Serenity Meditation

Many of us are familiar with the "Serenity Prayer": "God, grant me the serenity to accept the things I cannot change, the courage to change the things I can, and the wisdom to know the difference." Prayer can be a wonderful form of meditation, but not everybody is into prayer or believes in a higher power. In this meditation, we can change God to the deity of your choice, address it to the Universe, or request this of ourselves. For this example, I will address this prayer to myself.

In a comfortable seated or lying position, gently close your eyes. Focus on your breath, inhaling through your nose and exhaling through your mouth. Allow your breath to fall into its natural, resting rhythm. When you are ready, repeat to yourself:

> I grant myself the serenity to accept
> the things I cannot change,
> the courage to change the things I can,
> and the wisdom to know the difference.

Once you have repeated this to yourself, reflect on the things that you can control in your life. You can control what time you wake up in the morning. You can control what you buy at the grocery store. You can control how you respond to situations. You can control how you respond to people. You can control how you respond to your thoughts. There is so much in your control, and that is what is important to focus on. When you're ready, open your eyes.

1. Make a list of the things in your life that you can control and another list of the things that you can't.

_____

_____

_____

_____

_____

_____

_____

_____

2. What obstacles did you face while practicing this meditation? Why do you think that is?

_____

_____

_____

_____

_____

_____

_____

_____

Key Takeaways

- Acceptance means acknowledging our emotions and situations for what they are and recognizing what we can and can't control.

- Acceptance does not necessarily mean we're okay with or like a situation.

- By practicing acceptance, we can reduce interpersonal conflict, as well as resistance and negativity within ourselves.

- By accepting inevitable stress, we reduce the amount of self-made stress we experience and our overall suffering.

- Nonacceptance results in the perpetuation of negative thought cycles; by challenging these cycles, we can rewire our brains to be more focused on the positive, reduce our emotional reactions, and increase our agency and autonomy.

Chapter 3

Practice Compassion

In this chapter, we'll take a deeper look at compassion. We'll explore what exactly compassion is, why we need it, how to use it, and why it can be difficult at times. We'll also take a look at some examples and exercises that illustrate how to use compassion in our day-to-day lives and examine whether that compassion is directed at ourselves or others.

What Is Compassion?

Compassion is the feeling of concern or care that we feel for others or for ourselves, and the urge to decrease their (or our) pain and suffering. Compassion is more than just a feeling, though. Compassion is best shown through action, and this is often how people respond best to it. I feel like compassion is one of the most powerful assets that we have as humans. Compassion has the power to build bridges, repair relationships, create positive change in our homes and communities, and offer a comfortable resting place for ourselves and for others. Some common definitions of compassion include the word *pity*, which has somewhat of a negative connotation. I prefer to look at compassion as less pity and more sympathy, empathy, and caring.

Sympathy and **empathy** are both key components of compassion. Sympathy is the care or concern we feel for someone who is in an unfortunate situation. Empathy is our ability to relate to and to actually feel the same emotions that someone else is experiencing. Both of these words have external connotations, in that they are often applied to how we feel about or interact with others. This is obviously a major part of sympathy and empathy, as well as compassion, but it is by no means the only aspect. Typically, it's a lot easier to show compassion to others than to ourselves. Is this the case for you? Why do you think that is? Sometimes we're in a situation where we show so much compassion for other people that we completely forget about ourselves and end up violating our own boundaries in the process. Both compassion for others and compassion for ourselves are admirable qualities, but like everything, there must be a healthy balance between the two and we should never sacrifice one for the sake of the other.

Examples of compassion toward others may include anything from listening to someone talk to offering to pay for someone's coffee to protesting in the streets for equal rights. Compassion comes in all different shapes and sizes, and that's part of what makes it so amazing. It doesn't always have to be shown in grand gestures or immense effort and sacrifice on our part. Sometimes the form of compassion that someone needs the most is a listening ear, a shoulder to cry on, or a hand to hold.

> To show ourselves compassion, we must attune to our inner selves and listen to what our mind and body are trying to tell us.

Self-compassion, on the other hand, can be a little more difficult. For instance, if we need to talk or vent about something, we can't necessarily provide that for ourselves and have the same result as when someone else provides it for us. What we can do, however, is respect our boundaries—that's the best form of compassion that we can show ourselves. This can include personal, professional, financial, emotional, and time boundaries. To show ourselves compassion, we must attune to our inner selves and listen to what our mind and body are trying to tell us. Sometimes our body is telling us to rest and sometimes it's telling us to go exercise, for instance. By paying attention to our own boundaries and respecting them just as we would respect another person's boundaries, we can practice everyday self-compassion.

Why We Need Compassion

Can you imagine a world without compassion? What would that look like? To me, that world looks very bleak. As I mentioned, one of our greatest assets as humans is our ability to care for others and ourselves. On a global scale, compassion is essential to the growth and evolution of humans as a whole. Let's consider what our world would look like without compassion toward the earth and our global community. I'm not naive enough to think that all people have hearts full of compassion and that our world is perfect the way it is, even with compassion present. However, compassion is what gets us closer to creating a world that works for all of us.

External compassion is the root of wonderful movements like the civil rights movement, feminism, fighting climate change, and generally creating a world that is suitable and just for *all* people. If we didn't have compassion, we would not look out for our fellow humans. We would not care about policies that did not directly impact us. We would not have gotten as far as we have today. However, we still have so far to go, and compassion is essential for creating that global community of support and love, rather than the "everyone for themselves" mentality.

Compassion allows us to work for the greater good and to create a world that we want to see and are proud of. On an individual scale, we may not be able to incite global policy change or reverse global warming, but it's those smaller, daily acts of compassion that inspire others and get us closer to our goal of a compassionate world. By taking time to care for another person or animal, to listen, to give, to share, and to welcome, we share compassion with others. In the best cases, a domino effect is created, leading those we have helped to act in compassionate ways toward others. If there is no domino effect (and sometimes there isn't), we still know that we did good for someone else and we helped them, even if we can't see the immediate effect. When we act in compassionate ways, we plant seeds for growth and kindness in that person, whether toward themself or others. We don't want to underestimate small acts of compassion, because it is with those that we grow as humans and as a society.

> No matter what stories your brain tries to tell you, you are worthy of self-compassion.

As mentioned, self-compassion can be very difficult, and many of us know what it feels like to live a life without self-compassion. We can attest that it doesn't feel great. No matter what stories your brain tries to tell you, you are worthy of self-compassion. It would be wonderful to live in a world where everyone showed compassion to us when and how we needed it, but unfortunately, that just isn't the case. We need to be able to rely on ourselves to provide the compassion that we need. For better or worse, we are stuck with ourselves for the rest of our lives, so we might as well be our own best friend and caretaker, and be as positive and healthy as we can. Compassion, be it for ourselves or for others, feels good. It makes us happy. It also allows us to look on the positive side of things, to practice and enact our values, and to help others or ourselves.

Compassion has a direct link to belonging. By showing compassion to others, we offer them a space to belong. By showing ourselves compassion, we create a space for ourselves to belong. We can't have belonging without compassion and acceptance of ourselves and our fellow humans.

Belonging Toolbox: Determining Core Values

Throughout this book, I talk a lot about values and ensuring that we're always moving closer to our values through thought and action. Knowing our values is a key component of making sure we live our lives as authentically as possible. In this exercise, rank the five values that are most important to you. I have provided some examples, but I encourage you to use the ones that come first to your mind. They don't necessarily have to be the ones you're best at, just the ones that you feel are most important in your life. There's no right or wrong answer. It's important to understand what our core values are because they direct the choices we make. When we live in accordance with our values, we feel more fulfilled. This allows us to understand ourselves better and offer ourselves more compassion.

EXAMPLES OF VALUES

Adventure	Family/friends	Peace
Ambition	Freedom	Pleasure
Autonomy	Generosity	Respect
Balance	Honesty	Responsibility
Beauty	Integrity	Self-acceptance
Compassion	Intelligence	Self-knowledge
Confidence	Justice	Service
Equality	Love	Trustworthiness
Fairness	Moderation	Wealth
Faith	Openness	Wisdom

RANK YOUR TOP FIVE VALUES
(ONE BEING MOST IMPORTANT)

1. Out of your top five values, are there any that you feel you're not doing your best at living out?

    _____

    _____

    _____

    _____

    _____

    _____

    _____

    _____

2. What are some small ways you can enact your values in your daily life?

    _____

    _____

    _____

    _____

    _____

    _____

    _____

    _____

3. Are there any values you wish were more important to you than they actually are? What are some things you can do to make those values more important to you?

_____

_____

_____

_____

_____

_____

_____

Staying Compassionate

Remaining compassionate in a world that doesn't necessarily value compassion is an act of courage. Every day, events or people will challenge our ability to be compassionate. The tough question is, "How can we stay compassionate when everything is pushing or telling us to be otherwise?" It can be tempting and very easy to ignore our compassionate selves and respond to an inconsiderate driver or a rude waitress. It takes a whole lot more effort to use compassion in those moments. Likewise, it can be challenging to practice compassion for someone who has hurt us. Like acceptance, compassion is not the easy way out. It is challenging and difficult, but so worthwhile.

When it comes to compassion toward other people, it always helps to remember that everyone has a story. The reckless driver is on their way to the hospital to see their dying mother. The waitress who is being short with you just had a miscarriage. Or maybe not. Maybe they're just people, like you and like me, trying their best on a hard day. We shouldn't limit our compassion only to those who have "valid" excuses. Whether their story is seen as legitimate or not, it is still their story; they are still human, like us, and are deserving of compassion. Every one of us has had a moment when we were not at our best, yet we are still worthy of compassion from others, and this is true for others as well. If we act without compassion toward someone who acts without compassion toward us, it doesn't get us any closer to where we want to be. All it does is perpetuate the cycle of non-compassion. We want to ask, "What will my actions say about me?" By acting with compassion toward others, regardless of their behavior, we do not continue the negativity cycle; instead, we show ourselves and others that we are to be treated with kindness.

As with everything, applying it to ourselves may be more challenging. Many people, myself included, are way better at being compassionate to others than to themselves. However, the tools remain the same. We need to remember that we're only human, trying to do our best. This world, and everything in it, is difficult, challenging, and scary. We don't need to make it even more so for ourselves. We are allowed to make mistakes, have off days, not always be at our best—we're humans, not robots. I find this especially hard as a therapist, as compassion is basically my job. I beat myself up sometimes if I, like other humans, have a bad night's sleep and have an off day. But why am I any less deserving of compassion than my best friend who also had a bad night's sleep? Or a child? Or an animal? We need to treat ourselves with the same level of kindness and care. You're not supposed to be a robot. That's what makes you so special, unique, and human.

> With compassion, we show that we value ourselves and others for being our true, authentic selves—whether good, bad, ugly, or anywhere in between.

Some may see compassion as a weakness, but truly, it's our greatest strength as humans. With compassion, we show that we value ourselves and others for being our true, authentic selves—whether good, bad, ugly, or anywhere in between. The way I show compassion says more about me than the people to whom I show compassion. If I want to find belonging in this world, I must act according to what I believe; that includes compassion, even when it's hard.

Belonging Toolbox: Loving-Kindness Meditation

This exercise will help you create your own *metta bhavana* prayer, otherwise known as a loving-kindness meditation. This kind of meditation is one in which you speak wishes for yourself, others, and the world out into the universe. I will provide the general script and you can choose the words to put in the blanks. The words you choose can be whatever you feel you or others may need. In the first stanza, pick different words for each line. Those words will be the same words used throughout the meditation. However, don't feel constricted by this. Your wishes for yourself may be different from the wishes you have for others. This is your meditation, so feel free to customize it however you see fit. This meditation is a great way to practice compassion toward ourselves, others, and the global community as a whole.

To do this meditation, find a quiet space and sit comfortably. Close your eyes and focus on your breath, ensuring that you're taking full, deep breaths that fill your lungs. When you're ready, recite the following to yourself after filling in the blanks with different words:

May I be *(example: happy)* _____.

May I be *(example: healthy)* _____.

May I be *(example: peaceful)* _____.

May you be _____.

May you be _____.

May you be _____.

May we be _____.

May we be _____.

May we be _____.

1. Why did you choose the words you did for your meditation?

   _____

   _____

   _____

   _____

   _____

   _____

   _____

2. How can you help yourself and others achieve those intentions that you made?

   _____

   _____

   _____

   _____

   _____

   _____

   _____

Everyday Compassion

A key component to maintaining everyday compassion is to challenge our automatic thoughts. Our brains are wired to think negatively and to form a judgment, but all that does is perpetuate the cycle of negative thinking. It doesn't do much to improve our relationships, foster belonging, or allow connection with others. For instance, what is your automatic thought when you see a homeless person asking for money on the street? For some people, their first response is making a judgment about how the person got to that point. They may assume the person is on drugs or maybe not really homeless. These are judgment calls that we don't have any evidence for most of the time, and these kinds of thoughts can prevent us from helping someone in need and showing compassion.

I'm not saying that you should give away all your money to people on the street. If you have the means and would like to help, of course, that is admirable. However, we can show compassion in small ways that cost us nothing. The people we make judgments about are humans, too. Are they not deserving of compassion and kindness? And perhaps even more so if they are suffering greatly? When we challenge our negative thoughts and judgments against others and remember that they, too, are human beings who deserve kindness—regardless of the choices they have made in their lives—we can respond with more compassion, even if it is just a kind word or a smile. This can be applied to everyone you come in contact with: the difficult coworker, the person working at the DMV, your neighbor—even yourself.

A lot of the time, we make these same harsh judgments about ourselves. If we make a mistake at work, we may chastise ourselves more than a supervisor does. If we gain weight, we may punish ourselves. All the while, we're forgetting that we are just as deserving of kindness and compassion as the people we meet every day. Here's a technique that I find helpful: If you realize that you're being too harsh on yourself, imagine you're talking to a small child, a puppy, or even your best friend. You wouldn't use those harsh words with someone else, so why are you using them against yourself? If you realize you're passing judgment on yourself for having a human moment, reframe and challenge those automatic thoughts. Doing so may not come naturally or easily at first, and that's okay. This is a process of rewiring your brain and the way it works. By thinking a thought, even once, you automatically increase the likelihood of having that same thought again. This goes for both positive and negative thoughts. By challenging the negative thoughts and responding with compassion, you're carving out new neuropathways in your brain and making it more likely that you'll respond with compassion in the future.

I mentioned in the previous chapter that my work with teenagers in the group home setting taught me a lot of lessons on acceptance. The same is true for compassion. A lot of the girls with whom I worked in the group home were not the most pleasant. Some days, I would come into work, and they'd be excited to see me. Other days, I would come in, and they'd be calling me every name in the book, threatening physical harm, and telling me I was the worst therapist ever. It was a demanding job, and I found myself experiencing a lot of compassion fatigue (a form of burnout in which it feels like your ability to feel compassion and empathy is broken).

However, what got me through those difficult times (aside from *a lot* of self-care) was focusing on those times when I was the only one the girls felt they could talk to, when we hung out together at the pet store and played with dogs, or when we colored together. It also helped to remember their stories. Like I mentioned, we all have stories and we all have demons. Try to remember this when dealing with difficult people: It makes it easier to respond with compassion, and it's usually those difficult people who need it the most.

My work in the group home also taught me a lot about self-compassion. When I was coming into work every day and being yelled at by six teenage girls, it was really difficult not to internalize the criticism and think, "Maybe I *am* the world's worst therapist." We face a lot of judgments in the world, and again, we shouldn't be making this life any more difficult for ourselves than it already is. Practicing compassion with myself helped me understand that the anger my clients were directing toward me wasn't actually about me. I focused on taking care of myself, talking with my supervisor, seeing my own therapist, and practicing a lot of self-care to help me recharge my emotional battery. I knew I needed to take care of myself in those moments when things got difficult at work. By practicing self-compassion, I could be a better version of myself and a better therapist, even when challenged by everything life threw at me. Self-compassion builds resilience and our ability to persevere through challenges.

Key Takeaways

- Compassion requires sympathy and empathy toward others and toward ourselves.

- Compassion is necessary to build a happier and healthier life, both on a global scale and on an individual scale.

- Compassion toward yourself is just as important and necessary as compassion toward others.

- Practicing everyday compassion may require challenging automatic thoughts and negative judgments toward ourselves or others.

Chapter 4

Overcome Negative Thinking

A common statistic floating around from the National Science Foundation is that roughly 80 percent of our thoughts per day are negative and 95 percent are repetitive. Whether those exact numbers are accurate I don't know, but what I can attest to is that we are inundated every day with bad news and stressful situations, which makes it extremely difficult to focus on positive thoughts. In this chapter, we'll explore ways to work on challenging negative thought patterns and reframing our mind to explore the positive alternatives. We'll examine the function of doing this and how it can help us feel better in our lives.

What Are Negative Thoughts?

Negative thoughts can vary greatly, and they exist on a very wide spectrum. They can be big or small, intense or passive, true or untrue. What they all have in common, however, is that they are—you guessed it—negative! I've mentioned that our brains are hardwired to focus on negative thoughts. Again, this is a safety mechanism designed to keep us alive and protected. Unfortunately, we as humans collectively have not evolved as much as we would like to believe, and we still have a heavy unconscious bias toward focusing on the negative. As wonderful as it is for our brains to do this and keep us alive, it's not always the best at allowing us to thrive—which we do through taking risks, exploring, and having a variety of experiences. Negative thoughts can hold us back from living our lives to the fullest, while positive thoughts can allow us to appreciate the small moments, be mindful and present, and embrace the unknown rather than shy away from it.

So, what constitutes a negative thought? A lot of the time, we don't even notice we're having them because they happen automatically and unconsciously. Usually these thoughts look like judgments, assumptions, or accusations that are often not based in fact. Part of my intake process when meeting with brand-new clients is to ask them what they feel some of their strengths and weaknesses are. About nine times out of ten, they find it much easier to come up with their weaknesses rather than their strengths. Plus, they tend to list many more negatives than strengths. When you look in the mirror, what do you tell yourself? Do you say, "Ugh, I'm so ugly," or do you say, "Hell yeah, I'm awesome!"? What you tell yourself makes a difference.

These snap judgments and passing thoughts may not take up more than two seconds of our day, but believe it or not, they matter. Thoughts thrive on patterns; by thinking something just once, you start to create a new neuropathway in your brain, leading to a thought pattern. If you tell yourself six out of seven days of the week that you're ugly, but on one day, you acknowledge that you're an amazing person, which of those neuropathways do you think will be deeper, thus creating a stronger pattern? The negative thoughts, of course.

Negative thought patterns are an example of **cognitive distortions**, and they can creep into our daily lives in so many ways. Other common cognitive distortions include **catastrophizing** (believing the worst-case scenario will happen), **mind-reading** (assuming we know what other people think or feel without them telling us), **fortune-telling** (assuming we know an outcome of something that hasn't happened yet), and **discounting the positive** (when we insist that positive things that we have done don't count or aren't as good as everyone else's accomplishments). There are plenty of other examples of cognitive distortions, but these are by far the most common that I see in my practice as a therapist. Become familiar with the different cognitive distortions so you can better understand which ones you use on a regular basis. We'll explore this topic further in this chapter and examine how to challenge our negative thought patterns.

A Negative Lens

Are you familiar with the term *rose-colored glasses*? That's when we see everything through an overly positive lens—everything becomes rosy and we may ignore red flags. The opposite behavior can also be true and is actually far more common. As mentioned, our brains are hardwired to be on the alert for negative things because the brain perceives them as threats to our safety and well-being. However, sometimes our brains can start taking this job way too seriously and color everything with a dark, negative lens. As with everything, we want to be looking at life through clear, uncolored lenses: neither rosy nor dark.

When we view life through a negative lens, everything becomes a red flag, threat, or attack. For instance, maybe you're unable to feel happy about a positive review at work because you think maybe they're just trying to be nice and they really think poorly of you. Likewise, negative things, such as a poor work review, can become even more negative. Receiving a less-than-stellar review at work may quickly turn into you labeling yourself as worthless and terrible at your job. Maybe you think you're about to be fired. Did you notice any cognitive distortions in those examples? We had both discounting the positive and catastrophizing. When we look at things through a dark-colored lens, we rely more and more on cognitive distortions to support our beliefs.

Generally speaking, if we're looking for something, we'll find it. This is a phenomenon known as **confirmation bias**, which, more simply put, means seeking out new data or information that confirms our previous thoughts and beliefs. Therefore, if we're constantly (consciously or unconsciously) on the lookout for the negative side of things, we'll nearly always find it. Let's say you have a big presentation at work that you're anxious about. Where does your mind automatically go? For me, it would be thoughts about messing up, stuttering, getting some information wrong, making myself look like an idiot—the list goes on and on. Nine times out of ten, we tend to ruminate on these possibilities, making ourselves more and more anxious. Now, I'm not saying to completely disregard the negative options. A lot of the time, we can experience healthy stress and use that as motivation to prepare and do good work. However, if we're *only* focusing on the negative side of things, what are we actually doing to help ourselves? If we only consider the negative possibilities, our healthy stress turns unhealthy. It no longer motivates us, and instead it can paralyze us. During these times, doing well on something is so far gone from our mind, it doesn't even seem in the realm of possibility. Because we're only looking for the negative options, that's all we find.

The phenomenon of focusing more strongly on the negative aspect of situations is called **negativity bias**, and this is another very common cognitive distortion. When we use this cognitive distortion, our mind tends to weigh the negative options as being more important than the positive ones. Likewise, our minds tend to ruminate more and more on the negative side of things compared to the positive. Keep in mind that our brains do this because they want us to survive. I don't want to make it seem like our brains are working against us! They are simply doing their job. However, some people rely too heavily on some of these survival mechanisms due to biology, environment, past experiences, trauma, and so on. This is why some people struggle more with negative thinking than others. And just because our brains may be hardwired to think a certain way does not mean that it's hopeless for us to work on rewiring those automatic thoughts and reframing our thinking.

It's not as simple as just "looking on the bright side," but it is 100 percent possible to unlearn the cognitive distortions we employ frequently and learn alternative ways of approaching situations. The first step of unlearning negative thought patterns is to recognize their function and why we use them.

Notice what situations you use them in and approach them in a compassionate, nonjudgmental way. Cognitive distortions are normal, and it doesn't mean your brain is "bad." However, alternative ways of thinking can lead to more positive outcomes, such as generally feeling better, and relieve a lot of stress and anxiety. We'll explore this further in the next section.

Challenging Negativity

People may have given you the sage advice to "just look on the bright side" or "stop being so negative all the time." They may also be shocked to know that it doesn't work like that. They mean well, but it's just not that easy. If it were, my career as a therapist would be nonexistent. I want to be very clear that I won't tell you to just "think happy thoughts" or that "everything will be okay." Ultimately, statements like these are, at best, just not helpful and, at worst, they can be downright insulting. It's likely that we have all heard these phrases at one time or another, and they're all examples of **toxic positivity.** I mentioned earlier that we don't want to be viewing the world through rose-colored glasses or through dark-tinted glasses. We want our viewpoint to be clear and unobstructed. Toxic positivity is when we slip on those rose-colored glasses, and it can be just as harmful as our darkest metaphorical sunglasses. Ideally, we want to be approaching our world from a place of neutrality, free to acknowledge both the good and bad in our life but being realistic overall.

We can employ this tactic in our daily life in many ways, particularly when challenging negative thinking and those pesky cognitive distortions. One way to challenge negative thoughts is to use our "what-if" thinking in a positive way.

Going back to the example of giving a presentation at work, you may be thinking, "What if I blow it?" A great way to challenge this thought is to instead think, "What if I nail it?" So rarely do we think about the positive side of things when thinking about all of the what-ifs. Simply by noticing the positive *and* the negative possibilities, we can slowly but surely restructure our thoughts about situations. Before, doing well wasn't even a possibility being talked about in your internal conversation. But by adding in a positive what-if, you're able to decrease the negative, toxic stress and increase motivation and hopefulness.

Another great way to work on challenging negative thought patterns is to ask yourself, "Where is the evidence?" Cognitive distortions are lies our brains tell us. We essentially make up stories that we believe are true and are realistic enough to be true, but most of the time, we just don't know. This is a helpful tactic when dealing with mind-reading, fortune-telling, negativity bias, discounting the positive, catastrophizing, and so on. We often don't have enough proof to back up our claim.

Imagine you're presenting your case in front of a court. I did this with a teenage client who was convinced that no one liked her and everyone was just pretending to be her friend. I asked her where her evidence was, and she was stumped. She had no evidence to back up this fear, except that one classmate had told someone else that he and my client were not friends. From that one comment, she had created a narrative that nobody liked her. I asked her follow-up questions about this: Did he explicitly state that he didn't like her or just that they weren't friends? And let's say he *did* say he didn't like her. Where is the proof that nobody else likes her? Are our sources reliable? Is our evidence hearsay? Is our evidence based on fact rather than opinion? All these are questions that we can ask ourselves when we find ourselves ruminating on a story that is not based on fact.

> You can tell yourself, "Yes, this is difficult, but I can do difficult things."

Applying this technique to fortune-telling, for example, we can still ask ourselves about where the proof is that something will happen. For instance, if you're fearful of asking someone out on a date because you think they'll say no, what are some helpful statements or questions you can use to challenge those thoughts? First, identify the thought/distortion. The thought in this scenario could be "I'm going to ask them out, they're going to say no, and I will be humiliated." The distortion is fortune-telling. You don't know that the person will say no until you ask them the question. What is the purpose of this thought? Your brain is trying to protect you from potential embarrassment and hurt feelings. Is it uncomfortable to be embarrassed and have hurt feelings? Absolutely. Is it intolerable? Nope. You can tell yourself, "Yes, this is difficult, but I can do difficult things." It's possible that this person will say yes, and you both could end up very happy. By allowing our cognitive distortions to take over, we lose out on so many potential wins just because we're scared of losing.

Belonging Toolbox: Challenging Automatic Thoughts

Let's practice a simple way that you can challenge cognitive distortions and, as a result, change behaviors. Very simply put, this is how our brains interpret a situation and turn it into a behavior:

| Situation ▶ | Thought ▶ | Feelings ▶ | Behavior |

This is called a *behavior chain*, and it happens without us even knowing it most of the time. This exercise will allow you to take a closer look at situations that trigger unhelpful, negative thought patterns, how they impact our feelings and behavior, and how we can challenge those patterns not only to feel better but also to do better. The following table is an example of this.

SITUATION	NEGATIVE THOUGHT	FEELINGS	BEHAVIOR
A friend is an hour late to your party.	They got in a car crash and died. (Catastrophizing)	• Panic • Fear • Sadness	• Crying • Calling friend obsessively • Ignoring other guests

SITUATION	ALTERNATIVE THOUGHT	FEELINGS	BEHAVIOR
A friend is an hour late to your party.	• They had to work late. • They are stuck in traffic. • They fell asleep. • They lost track of time. Ultimately, I have no idea what happened, so I should not react as if I know.	• Possible annoyance but also under-standing • Much calmer	• Texting friend to see what's up • Being able to enjoy time with other guests

SITUATION	NEGATIVE THOUGHT	FEELINGS	BEHAVIOR
You are planning to ask someone out on a date.	They will say no, and I will be embarrassed. (Fortune-telling)	• Fear • Shame • Urge to avoid	You're too nervous to ask them out—an opportunity is missed.

SITUATION	ALTERNATIVE THOUGHT	FEELINGS	BEHAVIOR
You are planning to ask someone out on a date.	They might say no, but they might say yes. I have to ask to find out.	• Nervous but not toxic stress • More confidence • Acceptance	You ask them out, they say yes, and you live happily ever after! Or not, but you're sill okay because you can handle uncomfortable emotions.

Both of these examples include stories that we could tell ourselves. The initial thought that usually occurs to us is negative, but it's not helpful, it feels terrible, and it usually prevents us from getting closer to our goal. The alternative thoughts are not toxically positive, but are realistic possibilities that are more likely to happen. They don't necessarily result in the complete lack of uncomfortable emotions, but they do result in a more rational viewpoint, calmer emotions, and usually a better and healthier behavior. To practice, fill in the blanks with your own examples, and work on reframing your negative thoughts.

SITUATION	NEGATIVE THOUGHT	FEELINGS	BEHAVIOR

SITUATION	ALTERNATIVE THOUGHT	FEELINGS	BEHAVIOR

SITUATION	NEGATIVE THOUGHT	FEELINGS	BEHAVIOR
_____	_____	_____	_____
_____	_____	_____	_____
_____	_____	_____	_____

SITUATION	ALTERNATIVE THOUGHT	FEELINGS	BEHAVIOR
_____	_____	_____	_____
_____	_____	_____	_____
_____	_____	_____	_____

JOURNAL PROMPTS

1. Was it difficult for you to come up with alternative thoughts for your situations? Why or why not?

_____

_____

_____

_____

_____

_____

_____

_____

2. What are some possible obstacles you can foresee when it comes to using alternative thoughts in your daily life? How do you think you can overcome the obstacles?

_____

_____

_____

_____

_____

_____

_____

_____

Everyday Positivity

Challenging our negative thinking on a daily basis is an essential step toward creating deep neuropathways to positivity. At first, this may seem challenging, and you may feel like you're constantly thinking about your thoughts—which, truthfully, can be pretty exhausting. Look at it like a mental workout. If you go to the gym and have a goal of lifting a bunch of weight, chances are, on day one, you won't be able to do it (and if you can, your goal is too easy). Our big goals are made more achievable if they're made up of smaller goals. To lift a lot of weight, you need to practice, train, and work up to it. The same goes for our mental training. To think more positively, we need to train our brains to do so. At first, expect it to be challenging, but like anything else, with continual practice, you'll see the benefits.

When it comes to belonging, negative thinking can get in the way and prevent us from reaching our goals. It's part of the human condition to try to avoid uncomfortable feelings, and a lot of the time, this keeps us stuck. Discomfort, however, is a part of life and not something you can avoid. It's part of that inevitable stress that we discussed in a previous chapter. Negative thinking doesn't necessarily make us feel good, but it does keep us comfortable. When we begin to challenge our negative thought patterns, we may experience discomfort. With discomfort comes growth and the expansion of our comfort zone, which is often very limiting. Most times, the stress brought on by the effort to avoid the inevitable uncomfortable feeling is worse than the discomfort itself. If our goal is to create more social ties, make more friends, and connect with our family more, cognitive distortions can make us feel like taking the necessary steps to reach out is just too scary for us to cope with. This is another lie our brains tell us. We can cope with uncomfortable things.

By using more positivity in our lives, we're also able to feel better about ourselves. We can challenge the negative thinking that we apply to ourselves or our circumstances. By doing so, we can increase our hopefulness, which in turn increases our motivation for action. When we feel better about ourselves and are not living in the stories that our negative brains tell us, we open ourselves up to new possibilities, and with that comes greater belonging.

> When we feel better about ourselves and are not living in the stories that our negative brains tell us, we open ourselves up to new possibilities, and with that comes greater belonging.

I once worked with a client who had significant social anxiety. She felt extremely isolated and had a lot of trouble connecting with others. When we dove more into what kinds of stories her mind was telling her, I was unsurprised to find that they were all negative. She rarely opened up to other people because of her belief that others were not interested in what she had to say. Instead, she would often fabricate stories to sound more interesting, but this just perpetuated her lack of connection with others. When she did speak to people in her life, she wasn't being her authentic self. I worked with her to challenge her negative thoughts. She was a little hesitant to believe that she actually did have something to offer others, but after much insistence, she bought into the homework of starting conversations with two other people *and* being completely truthful throughout the conversations.

When I saw her in our following session, she was delighted to tell me that she had exceeded the expectations of two conversations and actually had five conversations. She also said that she found it so much easier than she thought she would and felt more connected than ever to other people. This example really illustrates how much our negative beliefs and thoughts can hold us back. Simply by challenging them and changing our behavior ever so slightly, we are able to build stronger and more genuine connections with others. Will it go perfectly every time? No, but it will also be so much less scary. In changing our behavior, we are also able to build our confidence and self-efficacy, in turn increasing our resilience and our ability to cope with uncomfortable emotions.

Belonging Toolbox: Developing a Gratitude Journal

Journaling is a fantastic option when it comes to general coping, challenging negative thoughts, or processing situations. However, it can be very difficult for some people to just freeform journal without any prompts or structure. A gratitude journal may seem like a cliché suggestion, but it's cliché because it works. Gratitude journals can help you feel calmer, shift your mindset toward positive alternatives, focus on what is really important in your life, and lower your stress levels. Consider journaling responses to the following prompts for two weeks. Afterward, reflect on how this practice changed your mindset and helped you focus on the positives in your life. I encourage you to continue on past the two weeks and maintain this as a regular habit to see the best results. Try to make your answers different each day.

- List three people you are grateful for.

  _____

  _____

  _____

- List three things you accomplished today.

  _____

  _____

  _____

- List three things you did today (or will do today) that make you feel good.

  _____

  _____

  _____

- List three things you are looking forward to.

  _____

  _____

  _____

JOURNAL PROMPTS

1. What was challenging about coming up with answers to the gratitude journal prompts? Why?

   _____

   _____

   _____

   _____

2. How do you think using your gratitude journal over the past two weeks has changed your mindset?

   _____

   _____

   _____

   _____

Key Takeaways

- Our brains are hardwired to survive, which often leads to us focusing on the negative.

- Negative thought patterns are called cognitive distortions.

- We can challenge cognitive distortions by thinking alternative thoughts, asking where the evidence is, and using positive what-if scenarios.

- Challenging negative thinking can help us feel happier and more confident, decrease toxic stress, and foster a sense of belonging with ourselves and others.

Chapter 5

Shift Your Mindset

Our mindset can be the difference between staying stuck and moving forward. The mindset that we cultivate matters, and it can be the delineating factor between growth and stagnation. In the previous chapter, we discussed how a negative mindset can prevent us from getting closer to our goals, whether we aim for success at work or improving our relationships. In this chapter, we'll discuss how to foster a growth mindset and how this can help us move forward to be the best version of ourselves. We'll explore what exactly a mindset is, its function, and why having a flexible and growth-oriented mindset is linked to belonging.

What Is Your Mindset?

A **mindset** is a basic structure of beliefs, viewpoints, and assumptions around which we structure our thoughts and behavior. I think of a mindset in terms of a house, Mindset Manor. The foundation and basic structure make up the mindset: They define what we fill our house with, where we put walls, and what goes where. Essentially, we fill in the blanks based on what structure we have. We can't furnish a one-story home with three stories' worth of furniture. Likewise, some things don't fit within the walls of our mindset.

There are two main types of mindsets: fixed and growth-oriented. A **fixed mindset** is rigid. It holds firm to its beliefs and assumptions to the point of resistance. Being steadfast can be a great quality, but there must be some give and take. In a fixed mindset, being open-minded is seen as a threat to homeostasis. Differences in thought or opinion raise red flags in our mind. Those who have a fixed mindset tend to stay stuck or stagnant in life because they don't allow themselves to be flexible or to adapt to changing times. Using the house analogy, this would be the equivalent to living in an outdated home that is too small for your growing family and refusing to build additions, remodel, or even move. The house is comfortable because you know it, but it just isn't working. When we have a fixed mindset, we often become stuck in what is comfortable and avoid challenges, thus halting our personal growth.

On the other hand, having a **growth mindset** means being flexible and open to other opinions, thoughts, experiences, and beliefs. Those with a growth mindset face challenges rather than avoid them, seeing them as excellent opportunities for personal growth. To have this mindset means to be always evolving into the best versions of ourselves. A growth mindset incorporates what we have discussed so far in this book: acceptance, compassion, and challenging negativity.

> Those with a growth mindset face challenges rather than avoid them, seeing them as excellent opportunities for personal growth.

A growth mindset fights the urge and the complacency brought on by staying stuck, and embraces the ever-moving and ever-growing environment around us. Going back to our Mindset Manor house analogy, this would look like changing and adapting our style to the times, adjusting the size as our family shrinks or expands or as our needs change, and accepting that we can move if we need to. We're not staying stuck in an environment that doesn't meet our needs just because it's comfortable; instead, we're challenging ourselves to take the next step because that's what is better for us.

Think about what type of mindset you have: Is it fixed or growth-oriented? A mix of both? In what areas are you fixed, and in what areas are you growth-focused? What challenges do you face by having a fixed mindset? What challenges do you face with a growth mindset? Spend some time reflecting on the areas in your life that are impacted by your mindset.

Power of a Growth Mindset

A growth mindset is a powerful asset to have. Who doesn't want to be the best version of themselves? With a growth mindset, that is what we're working toward. Of course, perfection is unattainable and, frankly, quite boring. With a growth mindset, we're not looking to be perfect; we're working on being healthy, fulfilled, and whole human beings, entirely capable of facing and embracing life's challenges. With a growth mindset, we can be flexible and prevent ourselves from getting stuck in situations that are no longer serving us and that leave us feeling static.

If I have learned one thing, it's that we need to be flexible. Years ago, I was a somewhat rigid person. If anyone out there is a subscriber to astrology, I'm a Taurus, which should tell you everything you need to know about me (i.e., stubborn!). As I have gotten older and had different life experiences, personally and professionally, I have come to realize that my rigid, unyielding mindset wasn't helping me in the least. I was alienating friends, I felt horrible emotionally, and professionally, I was at best mediocre. Challenges seemed insurmountable and scary rather than something to be embraced. At that time, I viewed life in very black-and-white terms (another cognitive distortion!). This thinking led to me getting stuck a lot because life is far from black and white—we as humans exist every day in a million shades of gray.

Our actions and beliefs don't directly lead to one outcome or another because there are so many variables at play. Likewise, my beliefs don't work for everyone, nor should they. The house I choose to live in is for myself, just as my neighbor's house is for them. With a fixed mindset, we tend to think that everyone should live in the same type of house. With a growth mindset, we appreciate having an eclectic neighborhood and respect the homes of others.

> With a fixed mindset, we tend to think that everyone should live in the same type of house. With a growth mindset, we appreciate having an eclectic neighborhood and respect the homes of others.

I have struggled with creating a growth mindset for myself and have helped plenty of other people along that journey as well. What can be very difficult about shifting from a fixed mindset to a growth mindset is that we really need to look in the mirror. We need to address those things about ourselves that aren't the best. It's essential to acknowledge the beliefs, assumptions, and judgments that our mind has "fused" to, and not all of them are pretty. We get these beliefs by watching and learning from other people's examples and survival mechanisms. A growth mindset takes in those setbacks and does not judge; instead, it acknowledges their function and what they have done for us. It takes them and shifts them into something useful.

Think back to our discussion of acceptance. When we resist acceptance, we end up creating much more suffering for ourselves. The same is true when we resist a growth mindset. We end up suffering more because we think our unhealthy relationship behaviors, coping mechanisms, and so on are correct. When we acknowledge that in reality, that stuff isn't working out for us, we shift our mindset to a flexible way of thinking, thus creating a growth mindset.

> When we're at our best, so are our relationships.
> A growth mindset is essential when it comes to
> cultivating belonging.

The power of a growth mindset is held in what it can do for us. Creating and cultivating a growth mindset increases general happiness. We experience less resistance in our lives and therefore less **cognitive dissonance** and discomfort. With increased acceptance of others, we improve our relationships. Likewise, acceptance of ourselves helps us thrive and be at our best. Acknowledging our unhealthy patterns or habits allows us to correct them and do better. A growth mindset shifts and adapts as it needs to, allowing us to be consistently evolving. When we're at our best, so are our relationships.

A growth mindset is essential when it comes to cultivating belonging. It moves us closer to our goals, while a fixed mindset keeps us stuck, all for the price of safety. What good is being "safe" when we aren't even happy? A growth mindset challenges us to expand our comfort zone further, to take the initiative and the risk to take the path less traveled. It requires humility and strength, which we all possess but sometimes underuse. We all have the capability to tap into those qualities and work to cultivate a growth mindset.

Belonging Toolbox: Thought Ranking

In this exercise, reflect on some of your beliefs that you feel are part of a fixed mindset. These can look like generalizations, assumptions, and judgments, but typically they are things we tell ourselves quite frequently. Then rate your belief in that statement from 0 percent (you don't believe it at all) to 100 percent (you wholeheartedly believe it, and nothing and no one could convince you otherwise). Next, identify your emotional responses to the statements, and rate that intensity on the same scale, from 0 percent to 100 percent. The objective of this exercise is to examine the thoughts that make up your mindset and to determine how you're responding to those beliefs.

THOUGHT	BELIEF, 0% TO 100%	IDENTIFIED EMOTION(S)	EMOTIONAL INTENSITY, 0% TO 100%
I am not good at my job.	20%	Sad, discouraged, hopeless, feeling like a failure	45%
My friends are just pretending to like me.	10%	Lonely, worthless, insecure	35%

THOUGHT	BELIEF, 0% TO 100%	IDENTIFIED EMOTION(S)	EMOTIONAL INTENSITY, 0% TO 100%

JOURNAL PROMPTS

1. How do the beliefs you wrote about impact your daily life?

   _____

   _____

   _____

   _____

2. What are some obstacles you can foresee in your journey toward exercising a growth mindset and challenging your belief system?

   _____

   _____

   _____

   _____

Dealing with a Fixed Mindset

Aside from keeping us stuck, a fixed mindset doesn't do much to help us evolve as humans, whether personally, professionally, emotionally, or spiritually. Generally speaking, a fixed mindset simply doesn't feel great. We remain static rather than dynamic, and often we become too comfortable and set in our ways. We all have the tendency to be fixed in certain things but not in others, such as being willing to grow within the confines of our profession but not pushing ourselves to grow in the relationships that we form. Sometimes our beliefs won't change, and that's okay. The goal of having a growth mindset is not necessarily to change what we believe; rather, the goal is to examine the beliefs that have held us down and kept us from progressing further—unhealthy beliefs that have hurt us more than they've helped. Likewise, we want to ensure that our beliefs do not cause any harm to ourselves or other people.

Everyone knows someone who can't be told anything. You may try to convince them of something and they just don't want to hear it. Is it difficult to genuinely engage with that person? When you leave an interaction with them, are you left feeling good about how it went? I had a teacher in high school who told me, "Don't be too open-minded or your brain will fall out." He is someone who exhibited a very fixed mindset. Open-mindedness was seen as a threat to the status quo and was too uncomfortable to be encouraged. Others' beliefs didn't fit within his worldview, so he discredited and dismissed them. Needless to say, he was not my favorite teacher.

One of the main reasons people keep a fixed mindset is that they can create a bubble for themselves where they're unchallenged; as long as they remain in this bubble and never have to admit they're wrong, they remain comfortable. I'll be the first to admit that it does not feel great to acknowledge that you were wrong about something or did something hurtful. However, we can't grow and move forward if we're not open to acknowledging the most genuine version of ourselves—good, bad, and everything in between.

By having a fixed mindset, we're just not our best selves, personally or collectively as a society. We disregard growth because it's too uncomfortable or frightening. By shirking the discomfort associated with growth, we're shooting ourselves in the foot in more ways than one. If we remain fixed, we're unable to adapt to the world and to others as they change and grow around us.

Think of all the technological and medical advances that have been made. Could those advances have been achieved if someone wasn't willing to challenge the status quo, if someone wasn't willing to take a risk and try something new? Likewise, societies that don't allow their policies to evolve as their people evolve historically aren't around for long. People and societies that stay stuck create policies that negatively impact others' human rights. They also create an environment in which racism, homophobia, transphobia, and other forms of discrimination run rampant. Humans are always changing, always moving, always on the verge of growth. A fixed mindset creates resistance to the flow of life, increasing our suffering and the suffering of our societies.

> To get the most out of our relationships and to find true belonging, we must allow ourselves to grow, to challenge those tired beliefs that keep us comfy, and to expand our mindsets beyond what is immediately in front of us.

When it comes to belonging, having a fixed mindset is not to our benefit. If people around us are changing and growing while we remain the same, soon we'll lose our connection with those people. Quite frankly, they will have outgrown us and will connect better with people who see the world in a similar way. We can also find ourselves not being fully genuine with others in our life, especially if we *believe* something to be true when it actually isn't. Thinking back to the example of my former client with social anxiety, she believed that she was uninteresting and didn't have anything to offer to conversations. This led to her being a false version of herself and failing to connect effectively with others. By challenging this belief and her fixed mindset, she took risks that may have been uncomfortable, but they paid off in the long run and allowed her to connect with people on a very real and genuine basis. She felt much more fulfilled in her relationships and better attuned to those around her. To get the most out of our relationships and to find true belonging, we must allow ourselves to grow, to challenge those tired beliefs that keep us comfy, and to expand our mindsets beyond what is immediately in front of us.

Belonging Toolbox: Challenging Our Inner Critic

The Socratic method is a way of politely arguing or challenging someone by asking questions. It is meant to challenge belief systems and to encourage critical thinking. This exercise will help you practice it within yourself (instead of practicing with others). It may feel strange talking to yourself, so step 1 is to draw your Brain Gremlin—that's what I call the little voice inside our minds that whispers all kinds of self-defeating nothings in our ears. I have people do this step first because it's much easier to argue with something that exists outside yourself. Your Brain Gremlin may reside in your brain, but it's not you. It's something completely separate from you and who you are as a person. (It will try to convince you otherwise.) In your journal or in the space that follows, draw your Brain Gremlin and fill in a few quick facts about it. For example:

- Name: _____

- Favorite saying: _____

- Greatest fear: _____

The second step to this exercise requires understanding that thoughts do not equal facts. Thoughts are simply words in our heads, and when we put stock in them and allow them to structure our mindset, they become beliefs. Using the Socratic method as inspiration, write down some phrases that can challenge your Brain Gremlin. Some examples:

- Would I say this to someone I care about?
- Where is the evidence that this thought is true?
- Is my evidence biased or reliable?
- How would I feel if someone said this to me in person?
- What are some alternative ways I could think about this?

_____

_____

_____

_____

JOURNAL PROMPTS

1. What did you find difficult or challenging about this exercise?

_____

_____

_____

_____

_____

_____

_____

2. In what ways can you use this method in your day-to-day life?

_____

_____

_____

_____

_____

_____

_____

_____

Everyday Growth Mindset

One of the most important tools in establishing a growth mindset is curiosity. By exercising curiosity, we acknowledge that we don't have all the answers and that our beliefs aren't inherently right or wrong unless they're based in fact. We also encourage growth and knowledge through curiosity. At my previous job at the group home, we often said, "Get curious, not furious." It was super corny, but wow, did it work! Every time someone (usually a client or one of the administrators) did something I disagreed with, I tried to ask myself why they would do that. By using this technique, I was able to work much better and more effectively with my clients and coworkers. I didn't have to agree with them or fully understand why they did what they did, but I did have to accept that they held a belief that was different from mine—and that's okay. This is a practice in incorporating not only curiosity but also acceptance. We need both to foster a growth mindset in our daily lives.

People will always do things that annoy us, but that does not mean we have to take those things personally, react, or even give them a second thought. Maybe they did what they did because we're a safe person for them (which was usually the case with my group home clients) and it was easier to take their anger out on us. Maybe they were having a bad day. Maybe we'll never know, and that's okay because it's not a direct reflection on us. When we use tools such as compassion and acceptance, we're better able to work with others and not only challenge our own beliefs, but also transform them into something positive and growth-oriented.

Another step to fostering a growth mindset, which should come as no surprise to you, is to watch the language you're using. We frequently use certain very common words that perpetuate a fixed mindset. First, we want to try to avoid generalizations. By using words like *always, never, every,* or *all,* we're engaging in false beliefs that are unhealthy. For example, something I hear a lot in my office is "I'm never going to get better." What emotion comes up when you hear that? To me, it sounds pretty hopeless. This way of thinking can create a self-fulfilling prophecy: We already believe that we won't get any better, so we don't even try. Another example is "I'm never going to get this done." This kind of thought discourages effort that may be difficult but entirely possible.

There are countless examples of using generalizations. Another way we do it is through labeling. I have a client who labels himself as "bad" or "evil." What makes a bad person bad? When applying that externally, we may say that perhaps they experienced trauma or had a bad role model, so they did a bad thing, as distinct from being a bad person. This is typically how we want to think of other people; this approach avoids generalizations and uses compassion. However, it can be more difficult to practice this internally. For my client who labels himself as bad, he can acknowledge that other people are not necessarily bad because they did a bad thing, but he believes that he is the exception to the rule. He holds a different set of standards for himself, and this is all too common. He's not a bad person because he labels himself so, and neither are you. Labels can be harmful because they erase humanity and variance in human experience, including our own.

Some other words we typically want to avoid are *should* and *can't*. By saying we should or should not do something, we're telling ourselves that there's a right and a wrong answer, and if we don't do the "right" thing, we feel guilty. For example, when you tell yourself, "I should work out today," but then you don't, how do you usually feel? I feel guilty, ashamed, insecure . . . the list goes on and on. When we reframe that to something like, "I would prefer to work out today," it becomes a choice. There's a choice that we would feel good about and a choice that we wouldn't feel as good about, but we've changed the narrative enough that it doesn't perpetuate guilt and shame.

The same goes for using the word *can't*. We only want to say *can't* when it's physically impossible for us to do something. For instance, I can't do a cartwheel right now. This is a fact. By saying, "I can't cope with this," we're selling ourselves short and telling ourselves that we better just give up and not even try. Not only that, but it's not a fact. Change your *can'ts* to *won'ts*, and it becomes a choice. Making it a choice encourages and motivates us to put in that bit of extra effort, to challenge ourselves, and to embrace discomfort and change in order to overcome a challenge. It's also important to use phrases such as *right now* or *yet*. You may have noticed I did that in my cartwheel example. I can't do it right now, but with practice and effort (and maybe some upper body strength), I could do it. Similarly, you may be feeling sad right now, but it's not forever. By changing the language we use, we're better able to cultivate a growth mindset.

Key Takeaways

- A growth mindset is one in which we are flexible and open to embracing challenges that bring change.

- A fixed mindset is a rigid way of thinking that keeps us stagnant and does not foster growth.

- We can develop a growth mindset by challenging unhealthy beliefs or thought patterns and by using growth-centric language.

- A growth mindset can help us genuinely connect better with others and accept ourselves more fully.

Chapter 6

Work on Self-Care

Self-care is an essential element to living a life that we're content with, bettering our coping skills, reducing unwanted symptoms, and improving our relationships with ourselves and others. In this chapter, we'll explore what self-care actually is and why it is so important. We'll also examine how to build a self-care routine that works for you and your specific needs, and learn how self-care helps us build better connections with others.

What Is Self-Care?

When I begin working with a brand-new client, I always ask about their self-care routine. Nine times out of ten, they think about it and say that it's "fine." When we actually dive into what self-care is and why it's important, they realize that they're not doing fine at all. People typically think of self-care at baseline as drinking enough water, sleeping, showering, and brushing their teeth. Sometimes people think of self-care as drinking a big glass of wine in a bubble bath while doing a spa-style face mask. All of these things are great options for self-care, but self-care in actuality is so much more than those tasks.

Self-care is, as I'm sure you've gathered from the phrase, caring for oneself. It's a simple concept to grasp on paper, but what does it actually mean? What does caring for oneself look like in reality? **Self-care** is anything that recharges our emotional battery. Life can be draining, so the purpose of self-care is to regain the energy we lose as we go about our daily life. I tend to look at self-care as existing in several separate domains: physical, intellectual, emotional, and spiritual.

Physical self-care is anything that exists in the physical realm of our being. This could look like physical movement, quality sleep, tending to our finances, getting a haircut, having a healthy relationship with food, keeping a clean living environment, and so on.

Intellectual self-care is anything that stimulates our mind. Work can sometimes fall into this category, as long as it's in balance with the rest of your life. It could also involve reading a good book, watching a documentary, or being creative.

Emotional self-care is the broadest. This can range from going to therapy to taking a bubble bath to spending time with friends. Emotional self-care can overlap a lot with the other areas, but the goal is to increase pleasure and decrease uncomfortable emotions.

Finally, **spiritual self-care** is what I consider the most neglected form of self-care. This can, of course, mean going to a place of worship or following a specific religion's tenets, but it doesn't have to. It can also involve yoga, meditation, mindfulness, connecting with nature, volunteering, connecting to your place in the universe, or connecting with people. Spiritual self-care focuses on those things that are bigger than what is in our line of vision; it transcends our mind and body and focuses on our spirit.

Now let's take a more dissected view of self-care. People usually realize that they're overdoing it in one area or underdoing it in another. The goal is to have balance between all areas in our life when it comes to self-care and not rely on one single form to recharge our battery. Self-care is also as unique as our fingerprints. What works for me will not necessarily work for the next person. Finding what forms of self-care work best for you can be a trial-and-error process, and you don't want it to become just another task on your list of things to do. We'll explore how to incorporate self-care into your life and how to attune to yourself to figure out how best to care for your specific needs.

Why Self-Care Matters

Self-care is more than just giving ourselves a break, though that is an important facet. Self-care also provides us the opportunity to care for ourselves the way we care for others. I have talked to so many clients, friends, family members, and strangers at the gym who have the same problem: They put other people's needs before their own. I myself have been chronically guilty of doing this. Self-care allows us to learn how to value our own unique needs and practice putting ourselves first.

For many people, self-care becomes something on their list of things to do that rarely gets done. We have this idea that self-care is something we can do to treat ourselves if we find the time or if we just happen to get around to it. It's not often that self-care finds itself as a priority on our list, unless things get really dire and we can feel ourselves spinning out of control. In those instances, self-care may be a last-ditch effort to prevent a meltdown. But to be most effective, self-care must be a consistent, daily effort.

Coping skills are what we use when we find ourselves experiencing an acute problem or strong emotion. While coping skills can sometimes look like self-care, they are distinct from it. Self-care is the daily maintenance we engage in that restores our emotional energy so we can better manage acute situations and rely less on our coping skills. Self-care is the preventive work, while coping skills are the in-the-moment work we do to manage a high-intensity situation.

Self-care is also an important element in getting to know ourselves. Generally speaking, it's not often that people take the time to tune into themselves and what they are feeling and to think about what they need. Engaging in caring for ourselves and putting in the work to meet our own needs can greatly improve the relationship we have with ourselves. This allows us to better manage stress, feel more energized, identify and process our emotions more effectively, and navigate life's ups and downs more successfully. By consistently asking ourselves what we are feeling or lacking, we improve our attunement to ourselves. We're also able to determine what kind of self-care we need.

Self-care is not one-size-fits-all. To effectively use self-care, we need to attune to ourselves. For instance, if you're feeling overwhelmed by how busy you are at work, you may need more of a relaxing form of self-care, such as journaling or meditation. If you're feeling anxious about something and have a lot of pent-up energy, something physical may be a good fit, such as going for a run. Not every form of self-care will fit every situation. Likewise, sometimes the best self-care you can do is rest, and it's important to listen to your mind and body when they're telling you to rest. Find what works best for *you*, and you can do that by listening to yourself. By putting this into practice and building this skill, you can use self-care more effectively and maintain a more consistently charged battery.

I have a client who deals with chronic illness, so her self-care tends to look a lot different than somebody who does not deal with the same experience. For instance, her focus on rest is even more essential, her ability for movement is limited, and she needs to be very mindful of what activities she engages in, so as not to exacerbate her illness or pain. However, that doesn't mean she is unable to engage in self-care. She just needs to ensure that she is fully attuned to herself and truly listening to what her body needs. It does make things more difficult for her, but self-attunement is something we all need to practice, in order to make sure that we are best meeting our own needs.

By taking care of ourselves better, we can also take better care of the people in our lives and have more energy to put toward creating stronger relationships with others.

Self-care helps us have more energy to afford to our relationships. If we're constantly walking around with our gas tank on empty, either we're getting the short end of the stick or the people in our lives are. We need to have enough energy to allot to the people who are important to us or those with whom we interact on a daily basis. We typically feel much more drained if we don't focus on ourselves first and practice self-care. This can impact our relationships because we're more likely to act snippy, fall short on friend duties, and be less checked in with our loved ones. Many of us really value caring for others, and we simply can't do that without taking care of ourselves first. It's not selfish to engage in self-care—it is necessary. By taking care of ourselves better, we can also take better care of the people in our lives and have more energy to put toward creating stronger relationships with others.

Build Inner Resiliency

Resiliency is our ability to bounce back from negative circumstances or events. Self-care allows us to build up our inner resiliency by improving our ability to increase our emotional energy and improving our self-attunement. When thinking of self-care, Maslow's hierarchy of needs often comes to mind. Psychologist Abraham Maslow created this theory in the 1940s to explain human motivation. The hierarchy is a pyramid that consists of five different levels, each dependent on the one before. The bottom level is the most foundational, and it consists of our physiological needs (i.e., water, sleep, food, breathing, etc.). The second level is safety, meaning having food security, safe housing, financial safety, and bodily

autonomy. The third level is love and belonging: our friendships, partnerships, and relationships with close loved ones.
The fourth level, which is second from the top, is esteem.
This means self-respect and respect from others, confidence,
achievement, and positive self-esteem. The topmost level in
the hierarchy is self-actualization—this means we are truly our
best selves, living a genuine life that we are proud of, and we
are overall resilient and whole human beings. Maslow the-
orized that each level is built on the one before it, and that
we can't reach a level without first securing the one beneath
it. For instance, we can't be fully actualized if we don't have
good self-esteem, and we can't have financial security if we
are lacking food to eat.

Maslow's hierarchy of needs is very important in understanding how self-care can help build resiliency. The hierarchy
breaks down what our needs are as humans and acknowledges
that we don't just need things like food, sex, and money to
be happy; it's so much more than those basic things. We also
need to feel safe and secure; to have strong, genuine relationships; and to be proud of who we are. We're at our most
resilient when all our needs are being met. Of course, some
of those needs might be out of our control, such as sudden
loss of employment, a relationship ending, or a safety concern in our neighborhood. However, you're not out of luck just
because some variables are out of your control.

Regarding self-care, like everything else in this world,
it's important to focus on what is in our control. If we focus
on what we can control in our lives—eating well, taking care
of our finances, spending time with loved ones, and talking
kindly to ourselves, for example—we can navigate challenges
and losses much better. This doesn't mean that we won't still
struggle and face challenges; it just means that by using our

resilience that is built on layers of self-care, we can sail the stormy seas with greater ease and confidence.

Another way that I look at self-care and how it helps build resilience is through the analogy of a bank account. In the account, we store our emotional energy. Some aspects of our lives make deposits of energy and some take withdrawals. Self-care should be the activities in our life that deposit energy into our bank account. Not only do we want to keep ourselves out of the red, but we also want to make sure our spending and savings are in order. By setting appropriate and healthy boundaries, we make sure the withdrawals are in check. Likewise, by regularly practicing self-care, we continue to put deposits into our account.

Of course, some deposits are worth more than others, and this can look very different for each person. By managing what withdrawals we make and how much we continue to deposit into our account, we're able to build up a reservoir of emotional energy. That way, when an unexpected withdrawal comes along (increased stress, a major loss, etc.), we have enough in our savings to bounce back. If we focus only on keeping our account out of the red and then are hit with an unexpected loss of homeostasis, we allow ourselves to go into the negative. By maintaining a strong savings account of emotional energy, we can recover more easily from life's challenges, thus building resiliency, and all of this is done through regular self-care practices. By practicing regular self-care, not only do we have that cushion when we experience a challenge, but we also can intervene more quickly and work on recovering from our losses.

Belonging Toolbox: Emotional Energy Bank Account

Jumping off from the idea of our emotional energy bank account, in this exercise, think about the things in your life that are withdrawals and those that are deposits. Additionally, consider how much each of those withdrawals and deposits is worth. You can use dollar amounts or whatever unit of measurement works best for you. The goal of this exercise is to challenge you to think critically about what in your life drains you, what energizes you, and where you might need to build better boundaries to control your spending.

WITHDRAWALS	DEPOSITS
Example: Having to clean my cats' litter boxes: –$5	Example: Meditating once in the morning and once at night: +$25

1. Where do you feel you need to set better boundaries in your life to manage the withdrawals you're making?

_____

_____

_____

_____

_____

_____

_____

2. What obstacles do you foresee in working to create a self-care savings account?

_____

_____

_____

_____

_____

_____

_____

Everyday Self-Care

As I mentioned earlier, so many people tell me that self-care is not a priority for them or that they don't have time for it. To that, I say: Change your priorities. I used to believe that I didn't have time for self-care either, but once I made a point to fit some into my daily routine—rather than frantically trying to jam it in on weekends—I noticed my energy shifting. Of course, I understand that it isn't just that easy; life is busy and full of obstacles. However, this world is so fast paced, and it has tainted the way we think. We're used to instant gratification, getting answers right away, and having constant access to everyone and everything all the time. This has made us believe that we always need to be *doing* and producing. If we're not being productive, then we're not worthy. Who else feels guilty the moment they give themselves permission to rest? That's because this world has made us believe that rest is to be earned.

The truth is, rest is a right and self-care is a right, and we all deserve them. The sooner you allow yourself to be at peace without thinking about what you "should" be doing or how you could have spent your time being productive, the sooner you can build self-care into your daily routine. We need to take the pressure and urgency out of some things on our to-do list. Some things can wait. Nothing is more important than your mental health (no, not even the laundry!). Remind yourself that you're allowed to rest and you're allowed to take care of yourself. Doing so is not selfish.

> Remind yourself that you're allowed to rest and you're allowed to take care of yourself. Doing so is not selfish.

However, I know the reality of life. Even after we get rid of the lie of productivity, we still have things that need to be done. We're still parents, partners, siblings, children, students, and employees. We each wear many hats, and life is busy. This is why it's important to establish a list of self-care activities that work well for you. We can't limit ourselves to a handful of activities. We need a selection—some to provide a quick burst of energy or focus, and some to help us wind down before bed.

I was recently working with a couple in serious need of some self-care, and every suggestion I gave was met with "We don't have time for that." When I get that response, I suggest that people start with things they're already doing and then make them into self-care. We all shower or bathe, so try making that time more mindful. Rather than just speeding through the process and falling into the rabbit hole of your shower thoughts, try to be mindful and present during the process. Engage all five of your senses (maybe not taste . . . soap doesn't taste that great) as best you can. Really try to focus on the peace of being alone, hearing the sound of the water, feeling the steam, smelling the shampoo, and really being present in the experience and process of the shower. By being mindful, we detach our mind from the hectic nature of our day-to-day lives and focus on the present. This can be a wonderfully relaxing opportunity to take care of ourselves rather than "just another thing we have to do."

Showers aren't the only activity you can do mindfully to create an opportunity for self-care. We can engage in anything mindfully. Another activity I like to recommend to people is cooking. We all have to do it, so we might as well make it work for us. Cooking is something that many people, myself included, regard as being horribly draining, but it doesn't have to be. We can make it a fun experience by switching things up, having different-themed days, trying new recipes, and cooking with a loved one. We can play some music, engage our senses, and really get lost in the process of what we're doing. There's no guarantee that this will work for everyone, but the advice is the same: Take something you already do and do it mindfully, add some fun or adventure, or make it relaxing. Even if you're pressed for time, you can still add some flavor into your routine and make mundane tasks a little more interesting and enjoyable.

Some other great forms of self-care that don't take up a lot of time include going for a walk, stretching, deep breathing, meditating, drinking tea, reading a chapter in a book, playing with a pet, and listening to music. Self-care doesn't need to be some huge undertaking. It could look like anything and take anywhere from a single minute to an entire weekend. The most important aspect of self-care is that we do it mindfully. I could be petting my cats, which is a great self-care option for me, but if I'm still focused on everything else I need to be doing and how stressed I am, it won't do too much for me. I need to be engaged and present and committed to the activity. Additionally, self-care can sometimes be what we choose not to do—such as checking our work email after a certain time or doomscrolling through social media. We can set boundaries and say no. To reap the fullest benefits, self-care must be done with intentionality and purpose. We all have the ability to do this and to make self-care a priority; we just have to allow ourselves to do it.

Belonging Toolbox: Self-Care Assessment

In this exercise, think about the self-care practices that are already established in your life. Brainstorm about what self-care activities you could begin practicing in the future. We'll break down self-care into four quadrants: physical, intellectual, emotional, and spiritual. The activities that you would like to engage in don't have to be ones you think you'll enjoy. They just need to be activities that you can commit to trying, even just once. You never know what forms of self-care will work for you until you try them! For instance, I used to absolutely hate meditation until I made the commitment to really give it a shot, and now I do it on a daily basis. Additionally, think about what percentage of your self-care, out of 100 percent, you dedicate to each column. Ideally, we want the proportions to be as balanced as possible, but I understand that some people may just respond better to some forms of self-care than others.

	PHYSICAL	INTELLECTUAL	EMOTIONAL	SPIRITUAL
Already doing				
Will try				

1. Was it difficult to come up with new self-care activities to try? Why or why not?

    _____

    _____

    _____

    _____

    _____

    _____

    _____

2. Do you foresee any obstacles that may get in the way of staying committed to self-care? What can you do to ensure that you stay on track?

    _____

    _____

    _____

    _____

    _____

    _____

    _____

Key Takeaways

■ Self-care is a way to build up emotional energy and resiliency, both of which can help us bounce back more quickly and more effectively from adversity.

■ Self-care is best when it is consistent and tailored to our unique needs.

■ Personal attunement is necessary to help us understand our needs better and engage in more pointed self-care.

■ Self-care can help us build better relationships with ourselves and others.

Chapter 7

Fostering Connection

In this chapter, we'll focus on how exactly to cultivate a life conducive to fostering connection with others. We'll cover why we need human relationships and the benefits they bring into our lives. We'll also dive into practical ways to take the necessary steps toward forming healthy and fulfilling relationships by making an effort in both physical or virtual communities. Finally, we'll discuss the various facets of relationships and explore the process of building a connection with others.

The Importance of Connection

There's no doubt that connection to other humans has been essential for the survival of our species. We've been dependent on other people for practical reasons throughout the history of humankind. As we have evolved and adapted, we have become reliant on other people for more than just survival; we need other people in our lives and relationships to fully thrive and reach the level of self-actualization we discussed in the previous chapter. Human relationships offer us opportunities to grow and develop into fully formed, healthy individuals. Without positive relationships in our lives, our brains start forming differently from the moment we are born. We need positive interaction to learn basic skills that we need to function but also to develop into prosocial and fulfilled humans. We learn best through seeing others do something and copying them. We learn how to be a good friend by being part of a friendship. We learn how to be in a relationship by having failed relationships. Our experiences and connections with others, good and bad, allow us to learn and develop. They educate and inform us on how to function in this world with other people.

> Our experiences and connections with others, good and bad, allow us to learn and develop. They educate and inform us on how to function in this world with other people.

Not only does connection help us develop appropriately and inform our behavior, but it also just feels good. This benefit cannot be denied—nor should it. It may be simple, but it's a direct benefit of connecting with others. Connection can help us feel less alone in difficult times. It can bring joy, adventure, and excitement. Connection offers the possibility of unconditional love and support. So many experiences and opportunities can be brought on through connection. Think of all the times in your life that you were left heartbroken. Think of when you suffered a loss or experienced a major disappointment. Now think of navigating those incidents alone. Reflecting on some of the most tragic times in my life, I can't think of those moments without being grateful for the friends and family who rallied around me and supported me. Think of those moments in your life that have brought you great joy and happiness. Think of every success and win, big or small, in your life. With whom did you share them? Again, I think of my friends and family. I think of those closest to me, the people with whom I can share my truest self.

Connection helps guide us through some of life's darkest times and some of life's most precious moments. Being able to share these experiences with others amplifies our joy, modulates intense emotions associated with hardships, normalizes and validates our experiences and feelings, and offers support, encouragement, and solidarity. At the end of the day, we are social creatures and we need relationships to survive and thrive.

Making an Effort

Strong connections typically don't just fall into our laps, unfortunately. Those who sit around waiting for someone to approach them or for a connection to just happen will likely be sorely disappointed. We need to make a conscious effort when it comes to creating relationships and forming new connections. This is usually the exact thing that holds people back from exploring their options in creating new relationships. Most people have no idea where to begin or how to even go about meeting new people.

I have worked with several clients who were new to town and had no idea how to meet people. Many of them had roommates, which did make it easier, but some did not. Not having that connection felt very isolating and suffocating, so much so that several considered moving back to their hometown or somewhere they had more connections. This is how important connection is. If we don't have it, it can literally drive us out of a new town, a new job, or a new apartment, back to where we already have a solid group of people to rely on. What most of these clients had in common was that they were genuinely stumped about how to meet people and make new friends.

Making friends as an adult is hard. Like, really hard. We no longer have the convenience of being in second grade and meeting the new girl in class and both immediately bonding over My Little Pony and the Backstreet Boys, how evil the math teacher is, or how we hate that one kid but think another is cute. Our interests have evolved along with us, and it can be more difficult to connect with people now because our interests are much less bright and shiny, and we no longer wear them on our sleeves. I've worked with plenty of people who don't even know what their interests are. They've gotten so stuck in the monotony of the day-to-day that they have little to no time for what they like and enjoy. When working with my clients who are struggling to find connection, the first step we cover is to determine what they're interested in. What do you like and find interesting? Don't worry about how you think others might perceive it. Chances are, if you like it, there's a whole community out there full of people who are also interested in the same thing.

There can obviously be challenges associated with finding those interests. As we get older, we become more nuanced as people and, in order to belong, we need to connect over more than just a favorite band or show we like. We also need to connect on values and shared experiences. A client with whom I work is Latinx and immigrated to the United States at a young age. She was the first in her family to attend college and own property. We frequently discuss how she often feels that she does not belong in her group of friends or in her neighborhood, which is predominantly white. Even her good friends are unable to connect with her, on the basis that they do not have a lot of shared experiences; they grew up having vastly different backgrounds. This has led to her feeling more isolated. Again, while her individuality is an asset, it can also make it more difficult to find belonging. However, if one person is feeling it, the chances are that many other people are feeling it, as well.

The second step, once you've determined what your interests are, is to go and find your people. You can't sit around waiting for your people to find you. Luckily, we have countless options at our fingertips to connect with people in our communities and in our global community. A great way to do this is through volunteering. Most of us have a cause that is near and dear to our hearts, whether it's fighting for equality, protecting animal welfare, feeding the hungry, working with children, or cleaning up the environment. Every community, big or small, has opportunities to volunteer; you just need to put in the effort to find them. This will allow you to connect with people who share a common interest and a common set of values (e.g., service, community, generosity, etc.).

If volunteering isn't your thing, don't fret because there are many other options. Facebook is an expansive community and has very specific groups, including individual interests or just people who are new to a city and looking for friends. Another fantastic resource is Meetup.com (as well as its handy app), which offers many virtual and live groups for all different kinds of interests. Don't see a group that piques your interest? Go make one! Like I said, if you have a certain interest, experience, or value set, the likelihood is high that a bunch of other people do as well.

In addition, several apps offer the benefit of finding new friends, such as Bumble (which is for all genders, and has a BFF option), Nextdoor (connect with your neighborhood), Hey! VINA (like Tinder but for female friends), Peanut (for mothers to connect with other moms), and Friender. These options are great because you all have a common, vested interest: to meet new people. This takes away some of the uncertainty and awkwardness of the situation. You're all looking for the same thing. With all these options, there's no excuse for not putting in some effort to make connections. Don't let your own mind get in the way of finding a new, supportive group of people.

Belonging Toolbox: Getting to Know Yourself

A key component to finding and fostering connection is understanding who you are as a person and what you bring to the table in terms of connection. This exercise is all about building self-awareness and asking yourself probing questions to better understand what your interests are and how you can apply that knowledge to finding connections with others. The exercise is simple: Just answer the questions that follow. Feel free to journal more about your answers if you feel the need to.

SELF-AWARENESS QUESTIONNAIRE

1. When you think of your ideal self, what does that look like?

   _____

   _____

   _____

   _____

2. What are some goals you have for the future?

   _____

   _____

   _____

   _____

3. What qualities do you bring to your relationships?

_____

_____

_____

_____

4. What qualities do you look for in other people when form-ing a relationship with them, either romantic or friendly?

_____

_____

_____

_____

5. Would you describe yourself as a homebody, or do you prefer adventure and travel?

_____

_____

_____

_____

6. What are your hobbies or new things you would like to learn?

_____

_____

_____

_____

7. What has prevented you from engaging in your hobbies or learning new things in the past?

_____

_____

_____

_____

8. Rank the following in order of importance as they are right now in your life: career, friends and family, recreation and leisure, money, health.

_____

_____

_____

_____

9. Would you like these to be ranked differently in the future, or are you happy with where they are currently?

_____

_____

_____

_____

10. What are some of your greatest strengths?

_____

_____

_____

_____

11. What are some of your weaknesses?

_____

_____

_____

_____

12. What are some things in your life that you would like to improve on?

_____

_____

_____

_____

1. Did you learn anything new about yourself by completing this questionnaire? What did you learn?

    _____

    _____

    _____

    _____

    _____

    _____

    _____

2. How will this knowledge help you build better connections with others?

    _____

    _____

    _____

    _____

    _____

    _____

    _____

Relationships Take Time

Along with effort, relationships take a great deal of time and patience. As mentioned, relationships don't usually just fall into our laps. If only they were that easy! (If they were, again, we wouldn't be here.) Building a healthy relationship has many steps and this can be very frustrating, especially if we've been struggling with finding connection for some time. However, to develop a sense of belonging in our relationships and truly cultivate healthy connection with others, we must acknowledge that this is a process and it does require persistence and patience. It may not be ideal, but in the long run, the relationships that we invest our time and effort in will thrive. Relationships are just like gardens: We have to tend to them and cultivate a healthy environment in order for them to grow and flourish. Likewise, we can't plant a seed and expect a fully formed flower the next day. All relationships begin as seeds, and it's up to us to help them grow. Flowers don't grow if they don't get the proper nutrients, and relationships don't grow if they don't get what they need either.

> Relationships are just like gardens: We have to tend to them and cultivate a healthy environment in order for them to grow and flourish.

So, what does the development of a healthy relationship look like? The short answer is that there is no one right way.

Each relationship is different because each person is different from the next. Building a relationship can be like peeling back layers of an onion. We start with surface-level connection and work our way inward. Superficial connection can look like sharing of common interests, lots of small talk, and understanding the other person's personality. This step can feel tedious to some, but it builds the foundation of connection and a relationship. As we spend time with the person, we continue to peel back layers. We learn more about them, and we reveal more about ourselves. Give and take need to be mutual; otherwise, the relationship will be one-sided and unfulfilling. This is why we need to go into forming connections with a solid understanding of who we are as people, what our strengths and weaknesses are, and what we're looking for in relationships. If those don't align with the person we're trying to build a connection with, that's okay. Forcing the connection likely will not result in a healthy, symbiotic relationship.

This can be very frustrating for many people. It's important to remember that we're not meant to connect with everybody. Finding friends is the same as dating: Sometimes we need to go through a few options before finding one that sticks. And even if we put in our best effort, the other person may not reciprocate or be in a place to open themselves up to forming a new relationship. This can feel very discouraging and trigger feelings of rejection in many people. If this happens, remind yourself that forcing a relationship is like pressing a round peg into a square hole: It's just not going to work. Also, remember that we can open up room for many different types of relationships in our lives. We can have our brunch friends, our work friends, our friends who can give us a great referral for a realtor, and our friends who show up with wine and ice cream without being asked when we're having a bad day. Sometimes one person can fulfill all of these needs, but most often, that's not the case.

Ask yourself what kind of relationships you have room for. When someone fits the bill for being a casual friend but not a best friend, reflect on how much energy you can give that relationship. It's also okay if you don't have room for someone in your life. That person just may not have the qualities you require to let them into your world. Remind yourself that just because it didn't work out with this one individual doesn't mean it won't work out with anyone else. The relationships that are meant to grow and flourish will do so as long as we put in the effort, exercise patience, and practice healthy relationship behaviors. Those that don't flourish simply don't have a place in our garden. That doesn't mean anything is wrong with your garden—it just means that the environment wasn't conducive for that particular flower to grow.

Belonging Toolbox: Self-Love Meditation

Meditation can be a great way to develop patience. When I first began my meditation journey, I had absolutely no patience. I couldn't wait for the meditation to be over, and my mind would be wandering to about a hundred other places. However, as I've continued on in this journey, I've noticed that my ability to sit with stillness in my meditation practice has carried over into my daily life. Also, it has become easier to practice using positive affirmations to remind myself to be patient and to accept what is coming to me, as well as to open myself up to new experiences.

This exercise will help you develop patience in regard to your relationships and the sometimes difficult and frustrating feelings that relate to them. Additionally, it will allow you the opportunity to practice using affirmations to remind yourself that you are worthy of connection and relationships. This is just a general outline, and there is room to make it your own if you wish.

To begin, find yourself a comfortable, seated position with your feet flat on the floor and your hands resting at your sides. I recommend setting a timer for about 5 to 10 minutes, but feel free to do this for as long as you like. I recommend playing some soothing background music or sounds to set the mood, but nothing that would draw your attention away from the meditation itself. Sit straight, as if the top of your head is reaching toward the sky, and gently close your eyes. Repeat the following:

I am worthy of healthy relationships. I am an important and essential piece of the universe, and I am deserving of good things. Relationships are hard, but I can do hard things. I am a confident and courageous person. I will open myself up to the possibility of allowing others to see my beauty and love me just

as I love myself. I have great things to offer. I am an interest-
ing and unique individual with so much to give. I cultivate a
healthy garden for my relationships to thrive in. I treat myself
with the same respect that I give to others. I move with inten-
tion throughout my day, and others can feel the light that I
offer. I am worthy of self-love and love from others.

Feel free to continue with this meditation by setting other intentions for yourself or for your relationships. You can also add any other positive affirmations. End the meditation when you're ready. Try to keep the positive energy cultivated through this meditation with you as you move throughout your day, and practice it on a regular basis if you can.

JOURNAL PROMPTS

1. Was this meditation difficult for you? Why or why not?

   _____

   _____

   _____

   _____

2. How will practicing this meditation help you remain patient and develop healthy relationships?

   _____

   _____

   _____

   _____

Everyday Connection

Each day is an opportunity to work toward building more connection. First, it's important to assess what obstacles in your life are preventing you from building the relationships that you want. Some of these may be within your control, and some may not. When I ask people what's holding them back from finding connection, most often they tell me that it's fear of rejection or judgment. To combat this, we must first be secure with our goals and values. Think back to the exercise on understanding what your core values are. As long as you continue to live by those values, you can feel confident that you're doing what is right for you. Not every person will understand that, but not every person has a significant role to play in your life. By having a secure sense of self and engaging in behavior that aligns with your true purpose, you can be confident in what you say and do and in who you are.

> By having a secure sense of self and engaging in behavior that aligns with your true purpose, you can be confident in what you say and do and in who you are.

Additionally, it's important to remember that everyone needs and is searching for connection. The actual likelihood of someone telling you, "No, I actually don't need any friends," is very low. Not impossible, of course, but not likely in the slightest. Chances are, others feel just as nervous and awkward about it. Like I said, making friends as an adult is hard, and I have yet to meet one person who does not struggle in some way with that. Sometimes it can help to acknowledge the awkwardness, even in conversation with others. By putting it out on the table, you no longer have to pretend you're cool as a cucumber, and this lets you be your genuine self. If you own it, that comes across as confident and humble, which makes you seem much more approachable and puts the other person—as well as yourself—at ease.

Another great way to practice building connection is simply to practice. Your goal doesn't have to be building lasting relationships; you can practice conversation skills and engaging with others more frequently. These can be strangers you're standing in line with, the grocery store cashier, your dentist, and so on. When we push ourselves to converse more and ask questions, we become more comfortable with it. Of course, not everyone will reciprocate conversation, even if we do seem approachable and kind. That's okay! It gives us practice trying something that doesn't work out. That's life. It may be uncomfortable, but the more we do it, the more we're able to see ourselves bounce back from it, and the less weight it carries. This allows us to approach other opportunities with more of an open mind and with greater confidence.

Finally, don't be afraid to be yourself, quirks and all. People don't like cookie-cutter friends. You are an entirely unique individual with a lot to offer, and it would be a shame if others were not allowed to see that. Not everybody will appreciate who you are or what you have to offer, and that is perfectly okay. This goes back to being secure in yourself and your values. As long as you value yourself, others will follow—and if they don't, be strong enough to set the necessary boundaries. This process can be slow and uncomfortable, but the alternative would not allow us to live our best and most authentic lives, full of love and connection.

I always think of one of my friends when I talk about the patience and openness needed to build connection. She and I met at the very beginning of grad school. Throughout the two years in the program, neither of us would say that we were friends by any means; we were simply two students whose paths crossed semi-frequently. Throughout those two years, she and I both felt a connection to the other, but each of us was too awkward to ask the other if they wanted to hang out outside school or do anything to develop the relationship. It wasn't until after we graduated that we began talking more, and we finally met up for a brunch date. It ended up lasting for several hours as we shared our passions for social justice and serial killers. We often look back on that and wonder why we didn't act sooner. We both could have used a friend during that time, but we allowed our insecurities to get in the way. This is a lesson in trusting your gut when it comes to building connection. If we had not taken the risk to reach out and share our true selves with each other, we would have missed out on the opportunity to build a beautiful friendship. And, if we had taken this step earlier, we could have had an additional couple years of friendship and adventure.

Don't let your mind trick you into thinking that others aren't interested or don't need a new friend, or that you're not special enough. You are, and you deserve strong connections and wonderful relationships. You just have to take the step to go out and get them!

Key Takeaways

- Connection with others can help us navigate through difficult times and amplify our joy in positive times.

- Building healthy relationships takes patience and effort, and it can sometimes feel discouraging.

- Self-awareness and valuing yourself are essential in cultivating connection.

- Countless opportunities are available to connect with others, either in person or online.

Chapter 8

Everyday Belonging

In this final chapter, we'll discuss all the tools and concepts that we have covered throughout this book. We'll explore how to tie them all together and put them into practice to cultivate belonging. We have covered acceptance, compassion, the power of positive thinking, how to challenge negative thought patterns, the importance of self-care, and the work that goes into building healthy, positive relationships. Now it's time to dive into how all these skills can foster a sense of belonging and improve our connections with others—and our relationship with ourselves.

Moving Forward

First, thank you and congratulations for getting to the end of this book. It was designed not only to teach you about useful tools for cultivating belonging, but also to provide you with an opportunity to take a deeper look into yourself and examine the ways that you may be perpetuating cyclical patterns of negative thinking that can prevent you from being your truest self. Introspection is not easy. When we hold the figurative mirror up to ourselves, we often see things that we don't like. I hope this book has encouraged you to accept those flaws and to practice self-compassion in how you treat yourself and in the language that you use when talking to yourself. All of us, without exception, have parts of ourselves that we're not proud of or that are maladaptive. The goal of therapy is to address these parts and develop them into healthier alternatives. As I was writing this book, it was my hope and goal to pack the tools that I use most often in therapy sessions with my clients into written words and make them accessible. Thank you for taking this journey with me, and I sincerely hope that my words have made a difference in your life.

Now we can tie together all the concepts that we have discussed throughout this book and apply them to cultivating belonging. In the first chapter, we discussed what exactly belonging is. Generally, *belonging* means being seen for our true self, and accepted and validated for that self, by another person or group. The biggest obstacle to belonging is the expression of our true self. So many of us have struggled throughout our lives with self-doubt, insecurity, or uncertainty about our own identity. Developing a strong sense of self is the first step to finding belonging. If we cannot express ourselves truthfully, we cannot be fully accepted by others.

This is where compassion and self-care come in. By developing a sense of compassion and understanding toward ourselves—even the bits that we don't like so much—we are better able to practice self-acceptance.

Self-care is an extension of compassion in which we recognize that we are worthy and deserving of love and care. Through self-care, we provide ourselves with the tools and kindness that foster personal growth and awareness. By first accepting ourselves and treating ourselves with compassion and care, we are more apt to extend those benefits toward others. Through self-care, we also have more energy to dedicate to others while still taking care of ourselves. Relationships are reciprocal, particularly when finding belonging, and we all need to ensure that we're our best selves in order to cultivate a relationship that is healthy and that offers a safe space for ourselves and others.

Through challenging our self-defeating thoughts and cognitive distortions, we are better equipped to live in a world that is not constantly overshadowed by doubt, assumptions, and judgments, either toward ourselves or others. By practicing gratitude and challenging our thoughts, we can dispel the negative thoughts that keep us stuck and stagnant. If we want things to change, we must do something different. To challenge ourselves and make a real difference in our lives, it's essential that we break out of what may be comfortable. When we live in fear of change or of leaving our comfort zone, we don't take any steps toward authentic belonging, and we prevent ourselves from showing the world our true personality. We don't have to listen to the lies that our brain tells us. We must push beyond doubt and cognitive distortions and take the concrete steps toward relationships and connection. Yes, it is hard. Yes, it takes effort. And yes, it is so worth it.

Throughout all of this runs the undercurrent of acceptance. We must learn to accept ourselves, accept others, accept our circumstances, accept what we can and cannot control, and accept and embrace discomfort. Only by doing this can we push ourselves into a space of growth and vibrancy. It is essential that we take those difficult steps in order to grow. When we cultivate and use a growth mindset, we are better able to foster connection and develop belonging.

Staying Resilient

Throughout the journey of cultivating belonging, it is important to remember that the journey is not necessarily easy or swift. Progress is rarely linear. You may experience several setbacks along the way, really struggle with a concept, or face disappointments. All of this is normal. It may be uncomfortable, but it's all part of the process. It can sometimes be helpful to practice mindfulness, learn to appreciate the journey for all that it is teaching you, and really be present in the moment. Every mistake or setback holds the potential for a learning experience. It's up to you to unlock that potential and not let it stop you. Unfortunately, there will never be a point in your life when you cross the finish line and declare, "I am now able to cultivate belonging 100 percent of the time and use all of these skills perfectly." As long as you're trying your best, which can look different each day, and taking steps toward the goal, you are headed in the right direction.

Because I'm a therapist, people in my life, both personally and professionally, kind of expect me to have it all together. I know the skills and I use them, so shouldn't my life be full of healthy relationships and positive energy? Like everyone else,

I have my own insecurities, fears, worries, boundary issues, and hang-ups. I may have a certain level of knowledge and training on a subject, but that doesn't mean I can implement it flawlessly. I still have times when I doubt the effectiveness of the skills I tell my clients to practice every day. I have days when acceptance is hard and I'm frustrated about this one little thing that is totally out of my control. I have relationships in which I struggle to set healthy boundaries and that leave me feeling drained and even angry. No one is perfect (not even myself, which I begrudgingly admit!) and the skills are not foolproof. Sometimes struggle and hardship will make the skills seem pointless, and you'll just feel tired. That's okay. Allow yourself to have those moments. You are human. Life isn't meant to be easy, but you don't have to make it harder on yourself.

So how do we maintain our resilience throughout all these ups and downs, and not allow ourselves to get discouraged? One of the first things we were told in graduate school was to always "meet the client where they're at." We can't come in with our own agenda and expect our clients to just understand and be cool with it. You can't be 12 steps ahead of them while they're still at the starting line. The same is true with how we treat ourselves. We're going to have days when our best is only 35 percent of our full capacity. Other days, our best will be 79 percent, and sometimes it'll be 1 percent. This is okay. If one day the greatest thing you can do to take care of yourself is get out of bed, pat yourself on the back because that's a step in the right direction. We don't need to be full speed ahead all the time. We need to allow ourselves to have those days when we struggle. What's important is that we get up and show up. All we need to be doing is heading in the right direction. Progress is progress, and it doesn't matter how quickly it comes, as long as you keep moving.

Life is difficult, and the tools we have covered in this book are sometimes hard to implement, but they are here because they work. I wouldn't tell you to use these tools and do these exercises if I didn't believe in them. All of these tools and concepts have been included for a reason. By regularly practicing the skills taught in this book, you can create in your mind a safe place to be. By accepting yourself and practicing compassion and self-care, you allow yourself to just be, without fighting against the current every day. By practicing the tools on ourselves first, we can extend ourselves beyond our comfort zones and reach out to others. It can feel daunting, but through practice, you are building up your resilience. You have the tools to bounce back from struggles and disappointments. You have the capacity to recover inside you already—these skills just help you clear the clouds and unlock that ability.

Belonging Toolbox: Creating Assertive Communication

A key component of relationship effectiveness and valuing your self-worth is ensuring that your communication style is appropriate. There are four communication styles: passive, assertive, aggressive, and passive-aggressive.

Ideally, we would like to display assertive communication at all times. This includes being firm and direct, clearly stating your needs and intentions, not being defensive or accusatory, being calm and confident, respecting the needs and feelings of others, and calmly expressing your own feelings. We need assertive communication to maintain healthy relationship dynamics, to set boundaries, to express ourselves appropriately, and to relate better to others.

Aggressive communication is when a person is loud or pushy, doesn't respect the boundaries of others, is dismissive of feelings, believes they are always right, and doesn't practice active listening skills.

Passive communication is just the opposite: People who use this communication style let others have all the power, have trouble saying no or setting boundaries, do not express or value their own emotions, assume that everyone else is always right, and are very conflict avoidant.

Finally, passive-aggressive communication occurs when an individual believes that others should automatically know their wants and needs. They become resentful and may act out in passive ways (e.g., purposely "forgetting" something to get back at someone). This is a manipulative form of communication.

In this exercise, I provide example passive, aggressive, and passive-aggressive statements, and your challenge is to rewrite each to reframe it into an assertive statement. Remember, assertive statements are collaborative and respectful. A good way to approach this is to start with "I feel" and then go from there.

Scenario: A friend asks you to drive them to the airport, but you have an important work meeting that you can't miss that day.

Aggressive: Absolutely not! Work is way more important than taking you to the airport. Why would you even ask?

_____

_____

Scenario: A coworker asks to borrow $20.

Passive: I only have a $50 bill, but you can have it. And keep the change.

_____

_____

Scenario: Your partner asks you to do the dishes.

Passive-Aggressive: Yeah, no worries, I can do the dishes. I usually do anyway. And I can see you're really busy watching TV at the moment.

_____

_____

1. What do you think is your primary style of communication?

   _____

   _____

   _____

   _____

   _____

   _____

   _____

   _____

2. What are some challenges that you face when using assertive communication? What do you think you can do to overcome those obstacles?

   _____

   _____

   _____

   _____

   _____

   _____

   _____

   _____

You Belong

As we close our journey together, I offer this simple reminder: You belong! You may not see it at this moment, but you have a spot in the universe. Billions of years of evolution, sunsets and sunrises, births and deaths, have led to this moment, right now, in the present, with you in it. That is not for nothing. The universe has molded itself into what it is right this instant, and that entails you being in it.

The objective of this book is to help make readers aware of their unique gifts—what they have to offer others—and learn how to use those gifts in forming relationships. I sincerely hope that my words have offered comfort and support, and that you've been able to practice the skills covered here and implement them in your daily life. This journey can be long and arduous, filled with uphill battles and what may feel like endless setbacks. This is not to discourage you but to remind you that you don't have to do this flawlessly. Expect that hardships will come and go, and know that you have the ability to overcome them. My goal in writing this book is to assist you in unlocking the power inside you to become the best version of yourself. It takes hard work and effort, but you have the ability to find your place in this world and to find people who offer love, support, and belonging.

Belonging Toolbox: Identifying and Overcoming Obstacles

The following exercise is often used in positive psychology practices to produce feelings of happiness and to encourage action in working toward personal goals. Respond to these prompts and reflect on what action steps you can take next.

- Imagine your ideal life. You have overcome all the things that you're struggling with now. Who is there with you? What does it look like?

_____

_____

_____

_____

_____

_____

- You are proud of everything you have accomplished and all the hard work you have put into building this life. What feelings are coming up?

_____

_____

_____

_____

_____

_____

- Tap into those feelings and try to feel them now, in this moment. What can you do to make this "ideal life" a reality?

  _____

  _____

  _____

  _____

  _____

  _____

- What are some action-oriented steps you can take to move toward your ideal life?

  _____

  _____

  _____

  _____

  _____

  _____

1.   Was this exercise difficult for you? Why or why not?

_____

_____

_____

_____

_____

_____

_____

_____

2.   What are some obstacles that could get in the way of
     you achieving the goals you have set for yourself? How
     can you overcome those obstacles?

_____

_____

_____

_____

_____

_____

_____

_____

Key Takeaways

- The skills and concepts discussed in this book are essential building blocks for forming the foundation of belonging.

- Through regular practice, these skills can create positive change in your life.

- Progress is not linear and demands patience, acceptance, and compassion.

- There is a place for you here. You are important, and you belong!

Glossary

acceptance: the process of acknowledging one's circumstances without trying to change them

affirmation: a positive statement used to challenge negative thinking

aggressive communication: communication characterized by antagonistic behaviors or words, such as name-calling, belittling, yelling, demanding, or violence

assertive communication: communication that is characterized by respectfully advocating for oneself, practicing active listening and validation, and setting healthy boundaries

behavior chain: a series of internal and external stimuli that influence one's behavior; a typical behavior chain follows the following pattern situation: feeling > behavior > consequences

belonging: a close and intimate bond with another person or group of people, brought on by sharing our authentic selves and accepting others' authentic selves

catastrophizing: believing the worst-case scenario will happen

cognitive dissonance: when one's thoughts or beliefs do not match one's actions

cognitive distortion: a negative thought pattern

confirmation bias: a cognitive distortion that occurs when we look for information that supports our viewpoint (e.g., looking for red flags while ignoring information to the contrary)

coping skills: techniques used to regulate intense emotional states (e.g., deep breathing, journaling, taking a walk)

discounting the positive: when we insist that positive things that we have done don't count or aren't as good as everyone else's accomplishments

emotional self-care: a subtype of self-care that focuses on bringing joy and respite to oneself

empathy: the ability to fully understand another person's feelings and to share in that experience

fixed mindset: holding firm to one's beliefs and assumptions to the point of resistance

fortune-telling: assuming we know the outcome of something that hasn't happened yet

growth mindset: being flexible and open to other opinions, thoughts, experiences, and beliefs

intellectual self-care: a subtype of self-care that focuses on stimulating the mind through thought, challenge, or creativity

mind-reading: assuming we know what other people think or feel without them telling us

mindset: a basic structure of beliefs, viewpoints, and/or assumptions around which we build our thoughts and behavior

negative thought cycle: a pattern of thoughts in which negative or unhealthy thoughts beget more negative or unhealthy thoughts; continues cyclically until interrupted

negativity bias: focusing more strongly on the negative aspect of situations

passive communication: a style of communication that is submissive and centered around the fear of upsetting others (e.g., always saying yes, taking the blame for others' mistakes, etc.)

passive-aggressive communication: a style of communication that is characterized by the avoidance of direct communication and confrontation, while still engaging in small aggressive behaviors (e.g., backhanded compliments, silent treatment, blaming others, etc.)

physical self-care: a subtype of self-care that focuses on caring for one's physical domain (environment, body, finances)

resiliency: the ability to bounce back from negative circumstances or events

self-care: the practice of caring for all of one's health and well-being

self-compassion: the act of emotionally and physically caring for oneself and tending to one's needs

spiritual self-care: a subtype of self-care that focuses on connecting to our spiritual selves and our role in the universe; this can be done through religion, meditation, volunteering, and so on

sympathy: the feeling of sorrow or pity for another person or their situation

toxic positivity: the belief that others should only have a positive mindset, thus invalidating their experience or emotions

values: principles that guide each individual's behavior; guiding forces or beliefs that direct choices

Resources

The Confidence Gap: A Guide to Overcoming Fear and Self-Doubt *by Russ Harris*
This book challenges us to change our mindset when it comes to our insecurities and to break the unhealthy behavioral cycles brought on by fearfulness and lack of confidence.

Daring Greatly: How the Courage to Be Vulnerable Transforms the Way We Live, Love, Parent, and Lead **by Brené Brown**
Discover the importance of being vulnerable and the fulfilling experiences made possible through vulnerability.

Eight Dates: Essential Conversations for a Lifetime of Love **by John Gottman, Julie Schwartz Gottman, Doug Abrams, and Rachel Carlton Abrams**
This book is perfect for bringing couples closer together through discussions across eight different topics.

The Gifts of Imperfection: Let Go of Who You Think You're Supposed to Be and Embrace Who You Are **by Brené Brown**
Discover how to make peace with being imperfect and live our lives in a way that taps into our inherent worthiness.

The Happiness Trap: How to Stop Struggling and Start Living **by Russ Harris**
This book explores why the search for happiness usually ends up making people even more unhappy and typically increases instances of stress, anxiety, and depression.

Love Warrior: A Memoir by Glennon Doyle

This book discusses how to confront pain and grief in our lives in order to become strong and powerful individuals.

Maybe You Should Talk to Someone: A Therapist, Her Therapist, and Our Lives Revealed by Lori Gottlieb

This is a memoir about being a therapist, being in therapy, and how to embrace being flawed and human.

The Reality Slap: Finding Peace and Fulfillment When Life Hurts by Russ Harris

This book offers tools to manage major life events, such as the loss of a loved one, and to navigate creating a fulfilling life despite the occurrence of unfortunate circumstances.

Untamed by Glennon Doyle

This book dives into how to stop living according to the expectations of others and society, and how, by doing so, we are able to be our fullest and truest selves.

References

Baumeister, Roy F., and Mark R. Leary. "The Need to Belong: Desire for Interpersonal Attachments as a Fundamental Human Motivation." *Psychological Bulletin* 117, no. 3 (1995): 497–529. DOI.org/10.4324/9781351153683-3.

Harris, Russ. *The Happiness Trap: How to Stop Struggling and Start Living*. Boston: Trumpeter, 2008.

Heatherton, Todd F. "Neuroscience of Self and Self-Regulation." *Annual Review of Psychology*, 62 (2011): 363–90.

Linehan, Marsha M. *DBT Skills Training Handouts and Work-sheets*, 2nd ed. New York: The Guilford Press, 2015.

Merriam-Webster. s.v. "relationship." Accessed March 12, 2020. Merriam-Webster.com/dictionary/belonging.

Over, Harriet. "The Origins of Belonging: Social Motivation in Infants and Young Children." *Philosophical Transactions of the Royal Society: Biological Sciences* 371, no. 1686 (2016): DOI.org/10.1098/rstb.2015.0072.

Reshetnikov, M. M. "Problem of Relation between Brain and Mind in Physiology, Medicine, and Psychology." *Journal of Psychiatry and Psychiatric Disorders* 1 (2017): 313–16.

Wickham, Jennifer. "Is Having a Sense of Belonging Important?" Mayo Clinic. March 8, 2019. MayoClinicHealthSystem.org /hometown-health/speaking-of-health/is-having-a-sense -of-belonging-important.

Index

About the Author

Adele R. Ackert is a licensed clinical social worker in the state of Illinois and lives in the Chicago suburbs with her husband, Brandon; two cats, Boo and Fruit Loop; and hamster, Poppy. She works primarily with children and adults who have experienced trauma or are suffering from depression, anxiety, or co-occurring mental illnesses. Ackert has previously worked in community mental health, primarily in the child welfare setting. When not working, Ackert enjoys traveling, any expression of creativity, experimenting with various cuisines, and all things spooky or Halloween-related.

CPSIA information can be obtained
at www.ICGtesting.com
Printed in the USA
JSHW010041260621
16139JS00003B/7